THE WORLD
DESERT FATHERS

STORIES AND SAYINGS FROM THE ANONYMOUS SERIES OF THE APOPHTHEGMATA PATRUM

TRANSLATED WITH AN INTRODUCTION BY COLUMBA STEWART OSB

—◆—

Foreword by
Sister Benedicta Ward SLG

—◆—

SLG Press
Convent of the Incarnation
Fairacres, Parker Street
Oxford OX4 1TB
www.slgpress.co.uk

© 1986 SLG Press

First Edition 1986
Second Edition 1995
Third Edition 2020

Fairacres Publications No. 95

Print ISBN 978-0-7283-0307-2
ISSN 0307-1405

Typeset in Palatino by Julia Craig-McFeely

SLG Press
Convent of the Incarnation
Fairacres   Oxford
www.slgpress.co.uk

Printed by
Grosvenor Group Ltd, Loughton, Essex

FOREWORD

There is a story of a monk who was asked to go to a monastery to speak to the brothers about salvation. In great distress, he went to his spiritual father and said, 'Father, I cannot do this. I have not even begun to live as a monk and how shall I speak to others?' The old man said to him, 'It is like this: at the Last Judgement, when we come to stand before Christ, we will see many sheep going joyfully into heaven on the right hand of Christ, and we will think that our place is to his left, as we know what we have deserved, but at the last moment, as we go with the goats, the sheep will look back and say, "But if they had not spoken to us, we would never have known Christ. Master, let them come with us" '.

There are two ways in which this is a fitting story for a preface to the translation presented here. First, because the experience of monastic life in the desert has these two sides. There are the words spoken and the actions performed. The first request of the ascetic was 'Speak a word, father,' a request for a verbal communication of divine life; the second request was, 'What shall I do to be saved? How can I respond in practice to this word?' In the companion volume to this, *The Wisdom of the Desert Fathers*, a large proportion of the material is about the 'words' given by one monk to another; in this volume a large part of the material is about behaviour, about what the monks did, how they received the words and acted upon them. Here are stories vividly reflecting the life of the monks and what is more, the busy life of the towns, the real world of Egypt in the fourth century in many of its aspects. Here is the gardener who prayed so deeply that when he heard the loud music of popular songs late at night, he only said, 'They are all going into heaven'. Here are two washerwomen, one of whom is seduced by a monk, while the other refuses a similar invitation and turns the monk concerned back to his vocation. Here are officials and magistrates mingling with the poor, the beggars, the blind; traders eager to cheat over their transactions in gold. Here are

i

lovers, a man who prizes the loyalty of friendship above passion, and another who learns true renunciation at the hands of a woman who returns his love. Here is one of the well-known stories of the desert in its simplest form: a monk goes to visit his sister who is a prostitute, and brings her away from a life of sin into the desert of repentance. Here is that endearing monk, a Tarzan of the desert, who ran freely with the antelopes, and found life in a monastery so difficult that he begged God to let him return to his antelopes. In this collection, the ideals, and dreams of the desert fathers are seen in action among other monks and among other Christians.

These stories are not modern biography; they are brief, anonymous anecdotes told, not to reveal character or outline action, but as edifying and instructive examples. They are a part of an ancient tradition of literature, in which words have a resonance beyond their surface meaning. They are addressed, like the sayings, to each one who reads them as part of the way to Christ, not simply as introductions to the person or event recorded. It is this sense of personal encounter which makes the quotation at the beginning of this Foreword appropriate in a second way for the translators of both volumes as they 'speak to others.'

BENEDICTA WARD SLG
Oxford, 1986

CONTENTS

INTRODUCTION

An old man said, 'The prophets wrote books, then came our Fathers who put them into practice. Those who came after them learnt them by heart. Then came the present generation, who have written them out and put them into their window seats without using them.'[1]

THE 'present generation' described by the worried old monk have been dead for nearly 1600 years. Fortunately, they had begun to write their own books in addition to those they put into their window seats, and so preserved the words spoken by this elder as he looked around him at what had become of the monastic ideal of his youth. His remarks strike the reader as oddly familiar, as if they have been heard somewhere before; and as prophetic, as if they will be spoken again. The words take life as they are read from the page. They are strange at first, yet they are strangely reminiscent. The translation of an ancient text makes possible such live contact between two vastly different times and places: in the case of this book, between fourth- and fifth-century desert monasticism and an English-speaking reader one and a half millennia later. The interest and value of the desert literature has been admirably described by others.[2] What follows here in place of an essay on the historical background of the sayings and stories of the desert fathers is a brief discussion of what it is to read these texts today, and how the age and character of the writings themselves may affect that reading.

The medium of translation might beguile the reader of an ancient Christian text into forgetting that a great deal of time has passed since that text, now so conveniently available in modern dress, was

---

[1] *Apophthegmata Patrum,* Systematic Sayings from the Anonymous Series, Nau 228, as translated by Benedicta Ward in *The Wisdom of the Desert Fathers*, Fairacres Publications, 48 (Oxford: SLG Press, 1975/1986).

[2] For further background information, see Benedicta Ward's introductory essays in *The Sayings of the Desert Fathers* (London: Mowbray, 1975) and *The Lives of the Desert Fathers* (London: Mowbray, 1981). The works in the bibliography below may also be consulted.

actually composed. But at some point a sharp reminder of cultural differences intrudes upon and even upsets today's pilgrim hopeful of a word from the elders of the desert. The sayings and stories of the desert are appealing for their directness and for their ability to make the crossing from fourth to twentieth century with a good deal of grace. Even so, some guidance or encouragement may be necessary to help the modern reader hear these words with the mindfulness they deserve. This introduction is written in the belief that the antiquity and complexity of a text, as well as the issues of interpretation surrounding it, can enhance its message rather than simply confuse the reader.

The translation is based upon three groups of early monastic sayings and stories which are among the several collections brought together in a Greek manuscript of the tenth or eleventh century. The actual contents of the manuscript are from a much earlier period, as far back as the early fifth century, when sayings and legends of Egyptian monks began to be written down lest they be forgotten. In time the manuscript was obtained by the collector whose name is attached to a major body of materials, now in the Bibliothéque nationale in Paris, known as the *Fonds Coislin*. This one is number 126 of that collection. It is a substantial manuscript of 353 folios, damaged at both beginning and end. What survives, however, is a very important witness to the tradition of the *Apophthegmata Patrum*, the sayings of the desert monks who through this legacy have helped to shape subsequent monasticism in both Christian east and west. Whoever compiled this manuscript has assembled a kind of monastic notebook. By the editorial standards of today the collection is chaotic, and in fact it consists of several distinct collections. It is evident that the copyists of another age were generally more concerned with gathering materials than with organizing them.

The Manuscript

It will be useful at the outset to describe, even at the risk of some confusion, the contents of Coislin 126. The first part of the manuscript is

2

an almost complete version of the Alphabetical Collection of *Apophthegmata*.[3] Coislin 126 is missing the Prologue and the first sixteen sayings, so one must turn to other manuscripts for the first part of the collection. The effort is well rewarded, for the Prologue to the Alphabetical Collection contains some interesting remarks about an earlier editor's methodology:

> Seeing that an account by many people is confused and disorganized, and disturbs the understanding of the reader since the mind cannot manage to contain in the memory all of the things scattered here and there throughout the book, we have set forth an alphabetical form of presentation. By this workable and simple method of arrangement, those who wish to benefit may do so. Thus the items concerning Abba Antony, Arsenios, Agathon, and those beginning with Alpha are to be found under *Alpha;* then items concerning Basil the Great, Bessarion, and Benjamin under *Beta,* and so on right through to *Omega.*
>
> There are other sayings and deeds of the holy old men which appear without the names of those who spoke or acted. These we have arranged in chapters after those arranged alphabetically.
>
> After examining and searching out many books, we have placed at the ends of the chapters whatever else we were able to find, so that deriving benefit to the soul from all of them, and delighting in those words of the Fathers which are sweeter than honey and the honeycomb, and living in a manner worthy of the vocation to which we have been called by the Lord, we may reach his kingdom. Amen.[4]

This alerts the reader to the existence of two kinds of sayings and stories: an Alphabetical Collection of attributed texts, and an Anonymous Series arranged topically in chapters (the Systematic Collection). The meaning of the last bit of the Prologue is unclear: does it mean that extra material was added later to the alphabetical categories and to the topical chapters, or to the chapters only, or as a third group following the Systematic Collection? Whatever the solution, by the time

---

[3] The Greek text of the Alphabetical Collection is in Migne's *Patrologia Graeca* 65:71–440. Migne's text is not based on Coislin 126, but is similar to it. An English translation may be found in Sister Benedicta Ward's *The Sayings of the Desert Fathers.*

[4] PG 65:73–6.

of Coislin 126 the neat structure established by earlier editors had given way to less rigorous organization.

Although the Prologue could be indicating the existence of one group of miscellaneous sayings following those arranged 'in chapters' (the Systematic Collection), Coislin 126 has two such groups, one preceding the Systematic Collection, and another, substantially longer, following it. The first has three discernible sections, and the second series, found after the Systematic Collection, has five. Thus, in place of the two 'layers' of anonymous materials described in the Prologue, the original texts and the supplemental ones, there are by the time of Coislin 126 actually nine.[5] The copyist of Coislin 126, and presumably his predecessors, continued the practice of collecting desert texts and adding them to those they already knew. They were not, however, terribly concerned about careful organization. The first three groups as found in Coislin 126 are: Section I, an assortment of eighty-eight sayings and stories from the desert tradition; Section II, forty-four anonymous *apophthegmata*; Section III, five stories under the heading, 'Concerning the Anchorites'. Those first three sections are translated here, and the fourth, the Systematic Collection, is to be found in *The Wisdom of the Desert Fathers*, the companion volume to this one.

From the start, then, the manuscript presents quite a challenge to the modern inquirer. However, the lack of order need not point to sloppiness on the part of the scribe, nor discourage attempts to learn the contents of the manuscript. It would be wise to pause for a moment to consider the apparent chaos of the text and to ask if there might be a way to use the very disorder of the manuscript as a means of recovering a sense of the scribe's intentions and of the expectations of his contemporary audience.

---

[5] The analysis of this and other Greek manuscripts containing *apophthegmata* was done by J.-C. Guy in *Recherches sur la tradition grecque des Apophthegmata Patrum*, Subsidia Hagiographica, 36 (Brussels: Bollandistes, 1962). The description of the anonymous texts in Coislin 126 is found on pp. 74–88. The three volumes of Guy's editions of the Greek text of the *apophthegmata* are available as Sources Chrétiennes, 387 (1993), 474 (2003) and 498 (2005).

The Growth of the Collections

Two broad stages of development lie behind the jumble found in Cois-lin 126. First, the original oral tradition of sayings and stories from and about monastic elders became a written tradition. This was a major change, involving not only the shift from a free-flowing manner of transmission, based on telling and retelling of stories, to a more static written form, but also a linguistic change. The vast majority of the desert monks in Egypt, the principal actors in these texts, spoke Coptic. The sayings and stories were preserved in Greek, the literary language of the period. (Coptic did not come into its own as a written language until later, and the collections of Coptic sayings that survive appear to be translations from Greek.) Chronology for these changes is elusive, just as it is for the processes which shaped the gospels in a somewhat analogous manner, but the start of large-scale transition from oral to written form is often placed in the early fifth century. This was a time of major upset in Egyptian monastic circles due to doctrinal controversies and barbarian incursions, and marks the end of the first 'Golden Age' of desert monasticism in Egypt.[6]

The second broad stage began once the sayings existed as texts which could be collected and copied. Revision and rearrangement were possible every time a text was copied, so that every manuscript constituted a unique collection. Although much or all of a particular manuscript's material may be found in other collections, its combination and ordering of the texts is distinctive. This process explains subsequent deviation from the simple order described above in the Prologue to the Alphabetical Collection. (Note, however, that the author of that version of the Prologue had already modified the collections by adding materials to them.) The notion that fidelity to an original source entails exact reproduction is a fairly recent assumption, and modern-day readers may be horrified at the lack of concern for 'accurate' transmission of early monastic wisdom. But a hand-copied

---

[6] See Derwas Chitty's study, *The Desert a City* (Oxford: Blackwell, 1966; R Crestwood, New York: St. Vladimir's Seminary Press, 1978), especially pp. 46–64.

5

text is still a living thing, especially when copied by someone who lives within the tradition of the text. Two traits become evident: first, the frequent modification of the original text in the interest of clarity or contemporary interest (or censorship, or entertainment); second, a lack of concern for a high degree of organization. This disinterest does not seem surprising in someone who sought to understand the text in a meditative rather than an academic manner. If sayings and stories are viewed as discrete bits of tradition, each deserving of leisurely perusal and reflection, the order in which they are presented becomes far less important than it is to a reader intent on synthesis and overview. A reading of the prophetic books of the Old Testament will provide a similar impression. The monastic community which was the likely audience for this manuscript was not primarily interested in systematic exposition, although the efforts at topical and alphabetical arrangement in the collections show that this interest was not entirely absent. Their first concern was having the tradition made available so that it might live again in them.

From the Fourth Century to the Twentieth

It can be difficult for twentieth-century readers who may have this same concern to appreciate the vast gulf which separates them from these texts and their compilers. The frequent appeals made in this century for a 'return to the sources' of Christian tradition often fail to acknowledge the challenges confronting someone who picks up an ancient text and expects an easy time of reading it with modern eyes. Fifteen hundred years, a different language, another part of the world make for difficulties in communication which even the best translation cannot eliminate. Remember for a moment the obvious minor differences between people of today and the inhabitants of the world depicted in this collection: the ancients knew nothing of such 'essential' items as aspirin and sugar, both later discoveries. They were without spectacles and false teeth. Travel was rare and difficult. Vocational choice was almost unknown. Birth and death were unmuted by hospitals and undertakers. Few people could read; for those who could, a personal library of even a dozen volumes was almost unimaginable. Their very conception of the world was different, and if they had ever seen a map, it depicted a flat earth arranged around the Mediterranean. If the Mediterranean was the centre of the world, the earth was the centre of the universe, and was orbited by the sun. Their conception of history and their lack of concern with 'accuracy' and 'objectivity,' suggested above, is only one clue that they perceived and communicated events of significance in ways quite strange to modern readers.

To these general remarks should be added some comments about monasticism in the fourth century compared to today. These texts are primarily anchoritic, that is to say, most of them are about monks who lived alone or in loosely-structured groups. Although some of the stories describe a cenobitic monastic environment in which the communal dimension was strong and expressed by a good deal of formal organization, these are unusual. However, for most monks in the west today the cenobitic pattern is far more familiar. Contact with the 'world' is far greater. Monks today are generally educated, often to an advanced level. Various sorts of work may entail a sacrifice of time available for solitary contemplation. All-night vigils are almost unheard of. Fresh foods are available, and fasting is moderate. Even the strictest monasteries provide physical surroundings unimaginable in ancient times. Traditional monastic virtues such as obedience and humility are seen in a more complex and nuanced manner, acknowledging modern studies in psychology. The desert has been interiorized, or even sometimes seen in the spiritual emptiness of frantic urban life. All of this may or may not evidence the decay or abandonment of an ideal; whatever one's judgement of the mainstream of modern western monasticism, its differences from the desert sources are simple fact. And yet these texts continue to be read.

The reason for this may have something to do with the very differences outlined above. The basic commitment to the Christian life shared by fourth century monks and modern Christians is obvious enough, but that in itself does not guarantee that ancient

7

words remain fresh today. For example, a seventeenth-century spiritual treatise is much closer to the present both in time and in theological culture than is the desert literature, yet is probably less likely to captivate a modern reader. This is the point at which the difficulties of the desert sayings and stories can enliven the reading of the text. The force of the sayings themselves often lies in their gnomic, or terse and aphoristic character. They surprise the hearer, and often they puzzle by virtue of their utter simplicity. Their purpose is to break through rationalization and complexity and to render clear what was opaque. In addition to this inherent quality, the strangeness of their original milieu and the perplexing disorganization in manuscripts can contribute to their ability to shake a modern reader from everyday assumptions about the 'way things are to be done'. And so, in a surprising manner, the aspects of the literature that frustrate on one level—often a highly intellectual, 'rational' one—contribute to their power on a deeper level of experience. It is as if old wineskins become new and full of new wine because their very antiquity makes them novel and fresh. Some of the texts in this collection may seem irrelevant, others even offensive, but most of them will compel comparison with one's own experience through the contrast in atmosphere. Within the tension of contrast, one may hear an echo or two.

The Translation

Having argued for the value of disorder, it nonetheless appears best in this translation to impose at least some order on the texts, mostly stories rather than sayings, found in Section I of the Anonymous Series. Broad topical categories have been devised and texts gathered within them. Each category is provided with a brief introduction which suggests the topic's significance in desert tradition. The anonymous *apophthegmata* of Section II are presented in their original sequence, with the addition of some anonymous sayings from Section I. Section III, the five stories 'Concerning the Anchorites,' appears at the end as in the manuscript. Throughout the translation the original position of a piece can be determined by consulting the number in parentheses. The topical arrangement is made with no pretence of providing a comprehensive survey of monastic themes, although a reading of these texts will complement a study of the more theological topics addressed in the Systematic Collection, translated by Benedicta Ward SLG.

A word about genre. Most of the texts in the first section are actually monastic *stories* rather pure *apophthegmata*, although there are both anonymous and attributed sayings scattered throughout. The stories differ from the sayings in that the essence of them is not a word or statement, but rather a situation and its resolution. These edifying tales are sketches of life in the desert that can provide a background for the pithier material of the sayings. The material in the collection draws from both anchoritic and cenobitic traditions, and includes a few stories from Syrian and Palestinian as well as Egyptian sources. Some of the stories are not actually about monks at all, but found their way into the collection because they touch upon subjects of interest to monks such as humility and chastity. Most of the texts are to be found in other collections, but as very few of these are accessible to non-specialists, the complete collection is translated here.[7]

The basis of this translation is the Greek text of the first four hundred sayings in the Anonymous Series published by Francois Nau in *Revue de l'Orient chrétien* between 1907 and 1913.[8] A French translation of the whole was produced by Lucien Regnault.[9] Sister Benedicta Ward SLG provides a translation of Section IV, the Systematic Collection, in *The Wisdom of the Desert Fathers*. This present volume, a translation of Sections I—III, complements her work.

---

[7] The tables in Wilhelm Bousset's *Apophthegmata* (Tübingen: Mohr, 1923) 107–10 and in Lucien Regnault's *Les Sentences des Pères du désert:* Troisième recueil et tables (Solesmes, 1976) 246–55 list the parallels with other collections.

[8] Volume 12 (1907) 43-68, 171–81, 393–404; 13 (1908) 47–57, 266–83; 14 (1909) 357–79; 17 (1912) 204–11; 18 (1913) 137–46. Four of the stories in Section III ('Concerning the Anchorite's) were published by Nau in *ROC* 10 (1905) 409–14. The fifth has not to my knowledge been published in Greek, and therefore I have translated it from the Latin text in the *Verba Seniorum* as found in Book V, Chapter 15, No. 52 (*PL* 73:963).

[9] Regnault, *Les Sentences des Pères du Désert: série des anonymes* (Solesmes-Bellefontaine, 1985).

I would like to thank Sister Benedicta and Abbot Jerome Theisen OSB for their encouragement, and Father Ivan Havener OSB for his advice on technical matters. Without the support of Brother Dietrich Reinhart OSB, the translation would not have been completed, and without Brother Michael Brady OSB, the final stages of preparation would have been far more difficult.

COLUMBA STEWART OSB
Saint John's Abbey
Collegeville, Minnesota, USA

Translator's note to the second edition: I have added a saying inadvertently omitted in the first edition (Nau 41, added to Section 6), and updated the notes and bibliography.

CHRONOLOGICAL TABLE OF EGYPTIAN MONASTICISM

249–51	Persecution by the Emperor Decius.
c. 251	Antony the Great born.
c. 292	Pachomius born.
300	Peter, bishop of Alexandria.
303	Edict of Persecution.
311	Martyrdom of Peter of Alexandria.
c. 320	Pachomius founds community at Tabennesi.
324	Constantine sole emperor.
325	Council of Nicea. Alexandria established as second in ecclesiastical importance only to Rome.
328	Athanasius, archbishop of Alexandria.
330	Amoun in Nitria. Macarius the Egyptian in Scetis.
337	Death of Constantine, as a Christian.
340	Foundation of the Cells from Nitria.
346	Death of Pachomius.
356	Death of Antony the Great.
357	Athanasius writes Life of Antony.
370	Basil, bishop of Caesarea. Writes Rules.
373	Death of Athanasius.
373–75	Rufinus and Melania visit Egypt.
379	Death of Basil.
381	Council of Constantinople.
389	Death of Gregory of Nazianzus.
399–400	Origenist controversy splits Egyptian monasticism.
407–08	First devastation of Scetis by Barbarians.
c. 412	Rufinus' History of the Monks in Egypt is completed; he dies Cyril, Archbishop of Alexandria.
419–20	Palladius writes Lausiac History.
431	Council of Ephesus.
434	Second devastation of Scetis.
444	Death of Cyril of Alexandria.
451	Council of Chalcedon.
455	Sack of Rome by the Vandals.

(Apophthegmata are written down and collected during the fifth century. Process of copying, editing, amplifying collections begins.)

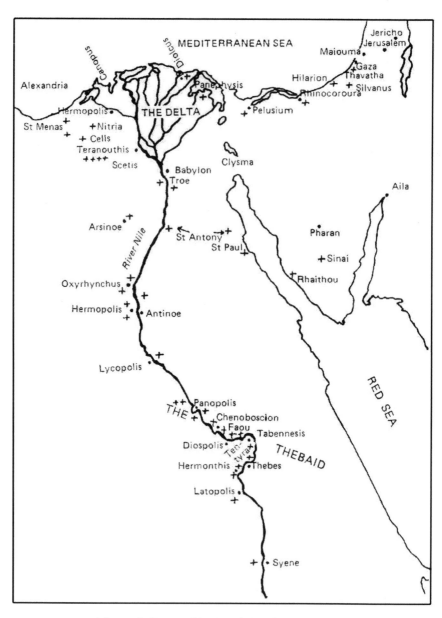

MEDITERRANEAN SEA

Jericho
Jerusalem

Maiouma

Alexandria

Canopus

Diolcus

Panephysis

Hilarion
Gaza
Thavatha
Silvanus
Rhinocoroura

Hermopolis
St Menas
Nitria
Cells
Teranouthis
Scetis

Babylon
Troe

THE DELTA

Pelusium

Clysma

Aila

Arsinoe

River Nile

St Antony
St Paul

Pharan

Sinai

Rhaithou

Oxyrhynchus

Hermopolis
Antinoe

Lycopolis

RED SEA

THE

Panopolis
Chenoboscion
Faou
Tabennesis

Diospolis
Hermonthis
Latopolis

Ten-
tyra
Thebes

THEBAID

Syene

Monastic Egypt, Sinai and Southern Palestine

12

SECTION I
MISCELLANEOUS STORIES AND SAYINGS

THE first part of the anonymous material in Coislin 126 appears initially to be an utter miscellany of stories and sayings, both anonymous and attributed. Closer examination reveals some clusters of associated texts, such as those about natural brothers (N 4–6), or about magistrates (N 37–9). Generally, however, this portion of the manuscript is a compilation of various sorts of materials with little regard for organization. They are presented here, therefore, in categories based on the clusters and affinities detectable in the series. Inevitably rather arbitrary decisions had to be made when assigning some texts to appropriate categories, and some of the categories are far broader in scope than others. They are here simply as an aid to the reader. The few anonymous *apophthegmata* found in Section I have been placed with those in Section II.

1. OLD MEN AND THEIR DISCIPLES

The fundamental human relationship in the desert was that between a spiritual father and a disciple, generally younger, who came to learn the monastic way of life. This relationship was in the first instance practical. Few people who came to the desert were prepared to undertake the work of monastic conversion without direction. A teacher was needed, one who could see into the heart of the novice to discover his intentions, and also through his heart to discern the course appropriate for him. There is also a theological truth at stake here; the elder-disciple relationship, founded upon charity, manifested the incarnational and deeply personal nature of Christianity. Therefore the spiritual father, or 'abba', necessarily had to teach by example as well as by word. The very existence of the apophthegmata demonstrates the value attached to the abba's verbal instructions; the monastic stories in this collection witness to the power of the elder's example and dispel the suspicion that an abba was less ready to demonstrate than to speak.

Equally necessary, of course, was the disciple's ready obedience in fulfilling a word or imitating an example. At times the obedience extolled in the desert literature may appear extreme or pointless; while it is difficult to apply modern standards to the desert, it is fair to say that a certain amount of exaggeration may be employed in order to make a point. Furthermore, paradigms of obedience, like other models, may be presented for the sake of inspiration rather than in hope of actual imitation. These stories depict both direction and obedience within the framework of the ascetical renunciation of possessions, of parents and siblings, of marriage and sexual activity, of society. These renunciations constitute the work of the praktikè, the first stage of monastic life when the counsel of an experienced monk is especially needed. The abbas in these stories, whether they be hermits or superiors of monastic communities, are directly involved in the struggles of their disciples while preserving the detachment necessary for true insight. They are not afraid to appear foolish or weak themselves in order to make the disciple see, as in story IV. Rather than figure as aloof oracles, these abbas lead their disciples by working alongside them, always tempering asceticism with charity.

I (17) There was a novice who wanted to renounce the world and he said to an old man, 'I wish to become a monk.' The old man said, 'You cannot.' The novice said, 'I can.' The old man replied, 'If you want, go, renounce the world, and come and sit in your cell.' He went off and gave away what he had, withholding a hundred coins for himself, and came back to the old man. The old man said to him, 'Go, sit in your cell.' He went and sat down. While he was sitting, his thoughts said, 'The door is old, and wants replacing.' He came back to the old man and said to him, 'My thoughts are saying, "The door is old, and wants replacing." ' The old man said to him, 'You did not renounce the world. Go, renounce the world, and stay here.' He went off, gave away ninety coins and hid ten coins for himself, and came back to the old man and said, 'Look, I have renounced the world.' The old man said to him, 'Go, sit in your cell.' He went and sat. As he sat, his thoughts said to him, 'The roof is old, and wants replacing.' And going back to the old man he said, 'My thoughts are saying, "The roof is old, and wants replacing." ' The old man replied, 'Go,

14

renounce the world.' He went and gave away the ten coins, and came back to the old man and said, 'Look, I have renounced the world.' He sat down and his thoughts said to him, 'Everything here is old, and a lion is coming to eat me up.' He told the old man his thoughts, and the old man said to him, 'I expect everything to come down upon me, and the lion to come and eat me up so that I may be set free. Go, sit in your cell, and pray to God.'

II (22) The fathers told this story: 'There was a superior of a cenobium, and it happened that his assistant, who regarded his duties lightly, left the monastery and went away to another place. The old man went to him constantly, urging him to return. But he was unwilling. The old man did this for three years, and so the assistant was convinced and he returned. The old man commanded him to go out and gather palm branches for mats. When the assistant went to do this, through the working of Satan he lost an eye. The old man was greatly upset, and began to remonstrate with the one who was in pain. The assistant said to him, "I myself am responsible, for this has occurred because of the troubles that I caused you." After some time he was freed from pain and the remaining suffering, and once more the old man commanded him to go out and collect palm branches. While he was labouring a branch sprang up and put out the other eye, again through the working of the enemy. As a result, he came into the monastery and remained quiet, doing nothing for the time being. The abbot was grieved once more, and because his own death was near, anticipating it he sent for the brothers, and said to them, "My call is at hand. Take care of yourselves." Each one began to say, "To whom do you leave us, abba?" And the old man was silent, and sent for the blind man to come alone, and he told him of his imminent death. And he wept and said, "To whom do you leave me, the blind man?" And the old man said, "Pray that I may have confidence before God, for it is my hope that on the Lord's Day you will be leading the synaxis." Within a few days of the old man's death, the blind man recovered his sight and became the superior of the cenobium.'

III (27) One of the old men sent his disciple to draw water. The well was a great distance away from their cell. He forgot to take a rope, and coming to the well he realised that he had not brought it. After offering a prayer, he cried out, saying, 'Cistern, cistern, my abbot said, "Fill the water jar." Immediately the water came up, and after the brother filled his jar, the water went back down again to its place.

IV (44) There was an old man who had a disciple, and when the brother was attacked by lust the old man would encourage him, saying, 'Endure, child, for the assault is from the enemy.' And the disciple said to him, 'I can endure no longer, abba, unless I actually commit the deed.' The old man dissembled and said to him, 'I too am attacked, child, so let us go together and commit the deed, and then return to our cell.' The old man had a coin and he took it with him. As they went towards the place, the old man said to his disciple, 'Stay outside; Let me go in first, and then you later.' The old man went in, gave the coin to the prostitute, and implored her, saying, 'Do not pollute this brother.' And the prostitute promised the old man not to pollute the brother. The old man went out and told the brother to go in. As soon as he went in, the prostitute said to him, 'Wait, brother, for though I am a sinner, we have a rule and we must fulfil it first.' Therefore she commanded him to stand beside her and to make fifty prostrations, and she at his side did the same. After the brother had made twenty or thirty prostrations, he was struck with contrition and said to himself, 'How can I pray to God while thinking about committing this filth?' And immediately he went out, unpolluted, and God, having seen the old man's labour, took away the attack from the brother and they returned to their cell giving glory to God.

V (46) One of the fathers related, 'There was a devout scholar from Theopolis [Antioch] who pestered a hermit, urging him to receive him and make him a monk. The old man said to him, "If you want me to receive you, go, sell your possessions, and give to the poor according to the Lord's commandment, and then I shall receive you."

Therefore he went away and acted accordingly. After this the hermit said to him, "You have another precept to keep, that you not speak." He took heed and for five years did not speak. Some people began to praise him, and his abbot said to him, "It is not good for you to be here, so I will send you to a cenobium in Egypt," and he sent him off. When he sent him he failed to say whether he was to speak or not to speak, so he continued to obey the command and did not speak. The abbot who received him, seeking a test to determine whether or not he was mute, sent him on an errand while the river was in flood, so that he would be forced to say, "I cannot cross it." He sent a brother after him to see what he did. As he approached the river, he knelt down, being unable to cross, and behold, a crocodile came and took him up and bore him across to the other side. When he had performed the errand and returned to the river, the crocodile again bore him across. The brother who had been sent after him, having come along and seen this, told the abbot and the brothers and they were astonished.

It happened that some time later he died, and the abbot sent a message to the old man who had sent him, saying, "That man you sent to me may not have been able to speak, but he was like an angel of God." The hermit then replied, saying, "It is not that he was unable to speak, but obeying the command which I gave him at the outset, he remained silent." And they all marvelled and gave glory to God.'

VI (53) An old man had a disciple who was his slave. Wanting to master him, he convinced him of the need to have perfect obedience. The old man said to him, 'Go, prepare a well-heated oven. Then, take the Bible which is read at the synaxis and cast it into the oven.' He went off and did it without a second thought, and when he cast the book in, the oven's fire was extinguished, so that we might know that obedience is good: for it is the ladder of the kingdom of heaven.

VII (72) There was someone in the cenobium who had his son with him from the world. The abbot, wanting to test him, said to him, 'Do not speak with your son, but treat him as a stranger.' And he replied,

'I will do according to your word.' And he did so for many years and did not speak with him. When his son's call came, and he was about to die, the abbot said to his father, 'Go now, speak with your son.' And he replied, 'When you command, we should obey the precept to the end.' And his son died and he did not speak with him. And all marvelled at how he received and fulfilled the precept with joy.

VIII (73) When an old man went down to Scetis, a brother accompanied him on the way. When it came time for them to part from one another, the old man said to him, 'Let us eat together, brother.' It was early on the first day of the week. When the old man arose on the seventh day, he came to the brother and said to him, 'Well, have you been hungry, brother, since we ate together?'. The brother said to him, 'No, eating each day keeps me from being hungry.' The old man said to him, 'Actually, child, I have not eaten since the last time we ate together.' When the brother heard this, he was struck with contrition and was greatly edified.

IX (82) The disciple of a great old man was tempted by fornication and went out into the world and married. The old man was grieved and prayed to God, saying, 'Lord Jesus Christ, do not allow your servant to be polluted.' And as soon as he was bound to the woman, he gave up his spirit and so was not polluted.

X (83) On the subject of evil thoughts he answered, saying, 'I exhort you, brothers, since we have refrained from the actual deeds, let us refrain from the desires as well. For what are we but dust from dust?'

XI (85) One of the fathers related, 'There are three things honoured by the monks, and which we with fear and trembling must pursue: the communion [koinonia] of the holy mysteries, the table of the brothers, and their washing of the feet.' He gave this example: 'There was an old man of great discernment. It happened that he was with many brothers, and as they were eating, the old man sat at the table and was attentive to the Spirit. He saw some eating honey, others bread, and others excrement. He marvelled inwardly and implored God, saying, "Lord, reveal to me this mystery, for the same food is set before all of them on the table, but it appears changed when they eat it, and some are eating honey, others bread, and others excrement." And a voice came to him from above, saying, "Those eating honey are the ones who sit at the table with fear and trembling and spiritual joy and who pray unceasingly, and their prayer rises to God like incense: therefore they eat honey. Those eating bread are the ones who give thanks when they partake of what God has given. Those eating excrement are the ones who murmur and say, 'This is good and that is awful.' One must not think of those things, but rather give glory to God and offer hymns to him, so that the scripture might be fulfilled, 'Whether you eat or drink, whatever you do, do all things to the glory of God' [1 Cor. 10:31]".'

2. MONKS AND SOCIETY

Monastic life is often described as consisting in the renunciation of the world. Properly understood, the statement may stand, but its starkness may lead to misconceptions. The caricature of the monk as a world-hater, unfortunately often supported by evidence from monastic literature itself, misses the point. The separation from ordinary society effected by withdrawal to the desert, or by the cloister, or by vows, is ideally less a quarantine than an opportunity. Nonetheless, the break with conventional human society is genuine, and these stories depict the tensions which can arise from the decision to choose the monastic alternative. Some of them are clearly cautionary tales for young monks, designed to keep them faithful to their monastic vocations for the sake of spiritual safety. Some, perhaps of special interest for modern readers, speak of the pursuit of virtue in the midst of secular society. Some of these tales have no reference to monks at all, but their inclusion in a monastic collection demonstrates that the virtues of seculars can be instructive even for those who have 'left' the world. One of the more humbling stories tells of a monk who found that the most virtuous person of all was not himself, nor even another monk, but a man who lived in the heart of the city, engaged in commerce, and was surrounded by all of the temptations which the young monks were taught to abhor. There is a lesson here for those prone to making too-neat distinctions between monk and secular (or, for that matter, between hermit and cenobite). Although one can never leave the world entirely behind, for a monk brings his past with him, the world can be seen in proper perspective, whether from the city or from the desert.

I (9) Abba Bessarion said, 'Someone once renounced the world who had a wife and also a daughter who was a catechumen but not yet a Christian. He proceeded to divide his possessions into three portions. Meanwhile, his daughter the catechumen died, and so the father gave her share, as well as his and his wife's, to the poor. He did not cease to entreat God on her behalf. And so a voice came to him while he was praying, "Your daughter has been baptized, do not lose heart." But he did not believe. Therefore the unseen voice came to him again, "Dig up her grave and see if you find her." Going to the grave, he dug and did not find her, for she had been moved to a place among the faithful.'

II (18) An old man said to another old man, who was charitable and brought monks and secular people together, 'The lamp shines upon many but sets its own top on fire.'

III (26) A brother from abroad sought counsel from an old man and said, 'I wish to return to my own kind.' And the old man said to him, 'Know this, brother: when you came from that land to this place, you had the Lord guiding you on your way; but if you go back, you will have him no longer.'

IV (37) Someone used to say, 'There was a young magistrate, a tax collector exceedingly handsome to behold, who was engaged in imperial business. He had a friend among the luminaries in one of the cities who had a young wife. When he went there, his friend welcomed him and he stayed in his house, and ate with his wife. He felt great love for his friend. Since he was often in close contact with them, the woman began to have thoughts about him but he was unaware of it. Because of her self-restraint, she revealed nothing of it to him, but remained steadfast in her suffering. It happened that, according to his custom, the magistrate went away and she fell ill from her thoughts and took to her bed. Her husband brought physicians to her and, after examining her, they said to her husband, "Perhaps she has an illness of the soul, for there is nothing physically wrong with her." Her husband sat down, pleading with her at great length, and saying, "Tell me what is wrong with you." She blushed and remained circumspect, and did not confess the cause. Finally she did confess, saying, "You see, due either to charity or to generosity, you brought here a young face, and I as a woman have suffered because of the magistrate." Hearing this, her husband fell silent. It happened that a few days later the magistrate came. The husband went out to greet him and said, "Look, my wife has been having thoughts about you." When he heard this, not only did he have no thought for her, but he was sorely grieved, and full of love for his friend said to him, "Do not be sad, for God will help." Going off he hacked off his hair, and taking some salve rubbed it over his head and face, up to and including his eyebrows. And so he destroyed the whole bloom of youth and resembled someone old and disfigured. He put on a head-cloth and went and found the woman lying down, with her husband seated beside her. When he came to them, he showed them his head and face, and said, "The Lord has made me this way." And when she saw him, changed from such a fine form into such deformity, she was amazed. When God saw his deed he freed the woman from the attack. Immediately she got up, rid of all those thoughts. Then the magistrate took her husband aside and said to him, "Behold, through God's work your wife is well, for she no longer sees my face." For, you see, this is what it means to lay down one's life for the sake of love, and to render good in return for good.'

V (38) One of the fathers said, 'There was a magistrate sent out on imperial business. He came across a poor man lying dead and naked in the road. Being deeply moved he said to his servant, "Take the horse and go on ahead a little way." The magistrate then went over, removed one of his own linen garments, placed it on the dead man lying there, and departed.

Some days later the same magistrate was sent out again on business. It happened that as he came out of his city he fell off of his horse and broke his foot. His servant brought him back to his house and physicians took charge of him. After five days passed his foot began to blacken. The physicians, seeing his foot blacken, agreed among themselves that the foot ought to be cut off lest the whole body become gangrenous and the man die. So they said to him, "We shall come in the morning and heal you." The sick man beckoned his servant to go out after the physicians and learn from them what they intended to do. They said to him, "Your master's foot has blackened and unless it is cut off the man will die. So we shall come in the morning and whatever God wills we shall do." The servant came to his master, weeping and saying, "They are planning these things for you." When he heard this he was grieved, and could not sleep due to his great despondency. There was a candle left burning. In the middle of the night he saw a man come in through the door, come over to him, and say, "Why are you weeping, why are you grieving?" And he said, "Sir, do you want me not to weep and not to grieve even though my foot was broken and the physicians are planning to cut it off?" The apparition said to him, "Show me your foot." And he anointed it and said, "Get up now and walk." The sick man replied, "It is broken and I am unable to get up." So he said to him, "Lean on me." And he leaned on him and walked lamely. So the apparition said to him, "You are still lame; lie down again." He proceeded to anoint him again on both feet. And he said to him, "Get up now and walk." He stood up and walked normally. Then he said to him, "Go lie down and rest." And he spoke some words to him about mercifulness, because the Lord said, "Blessed are the merciful, for they shall have mercy shown to them" [Matt. 5:7] but "Merciless is the judgement of the one not showing mercy" [cf. Matt. 18:35]. And then he said to him, "Be saved." The magistrate said, "Are you leaving?" He replied, "What do you want in addition to regaining your health?" The magistrate said to him, "By the God who has sent you, tell me who you are." He replied, "Look at me. Certainly you recognize this linen cloth?" And he said, "Yes, sir, it is mine." The other replied, "I am he whom you saw dead and cast off in the road, and you gave me your garment. And so God sent me to heal you. Therefore give thanks for all things to God." And he left by way of the door through which he came. And the magistrate, having been healed, glorified God, the cause of all good.'

VI (39) Another magistrate, returning to Constantinople from Palestine, came across a blind man without a guide on the road near Tyre. Hearing the noise made by the horsemen, the blind man turned off of the road a bit, extended his hands, and spoke in a wretched and poor fashion, begging alms from the magistrate. Thinking about it, the magistrate drew up opposite him, a little distance away, and was filled with pity. He stayed his horse, took a coin out of his change purse, went over to the poor man and offered the coin to him. He received it and blessed him, saying, 'I believe by God that this kindness will save you from a trial.' The magistrate received this prayer with great trust. He went on into the city and found the governor there with some soldiers who were pleading with him to give them a boat. But they were denied their request. When they saw the magistrate, the soldiers pleaded with him to ask the governor to give them a boat in which to travel out of the city. Persuaded by their entreaty, he went to the governor, and after speaking to him about the post horses the governor might give him, asked about the soldiers' request. As a result the governor said to the soldiers, in a kindly manner", 'If you want me to discharge you, persuade the magistrate to sail with you, and you shall be discharged immediately.' Hearing this, they all set about urging the magistrate to agree to travel with them. Because he agreed, the governor gave them a boat.

The magistrate and the soldiers then set sail, benefitting from a favourable wind. It happened in the night that the magistrate was having stomach trouble and needed to get up. While at the side of the boat he was struck by the rigging and fell into the sea. The sailors could hear his fall but because it was night and there was a strong wind they were unable to pull him out. The magistrate was carried off upon the water, expecting to die, but just at that moment, by the will of God, a boat was passing and those in the boat saw him, brought him up on board, and they arrived at the same city to which the soldiers had gone.

After landing, the sailors from both boats went to a certain tavern. It happened that one of the sailors from the boat out of which the magistrate had fallen, thinking about him, lamented and said, 'But what has come of that magistrate?' Hearing this, a sailor from the other boat asked what kind of magistrate he was mourning, and then, because he knew the true story, told them, 'We saved him and we have him with us.' When they found this out, the others rejoiced and went and got him. The magistrate told them, 'The blind man to whom I gave a coin on the road carried me while he walked upon the water.' When they heard this they gave glory to the Saviour and to God.

From this we understand that mercy does not pass away out of sight, for God repays the merciful in time of need. Therefore, in accordance with sacred scripture, 'Let us not desist from doing good for the needy whenever our hand is able to offer assistance.' [cf. Deut. 15:11].

VII (47) Someone said, 'There was a rich man in Alexandria who became ill. Fearful of death, he took thirty pounds of gold and gave it to the poor. It so happened that he was restored to health and he began to regret what he had done. He had a devout friend, and he ventured to say to him, "I regret what I did." And he said to him, "You ought rather to rejoice, having given it to Christ." But he was not consoled. So his friend said to him, "Here are thirty pounds"—for he was a rich man himself—"go into the church of St. Menas and say, 'It is not I who have fulfilled the commandment, but it is he,' and then take the gold." And when they went into St. Menas', he spoke the words and took the thirty pounds. As he was going out the door, he died. They said to the owner of the gold coins, "Take what is yours." And he said, "Let it be forbidden me by God, for when I gave them to Christ, they became his, so let them be given to the poor." Those who heard of these events were struck with awe, and they gave glory to God for the man's offering.'

VIII (48) There was a keeper of scales in a city and someone of the town came to him bringing a seal worth five hundred coins, and said to him, 'Take this seal and whenever I have need you can give me part of its value.' There was no one present there when he gave him the seal. One of the luminaries of the town, strolling outside of the scale-house, heard and saw that he gave him the seal. The keeper of scales did not know that he had overheard. After a few days had passed, the one who had given the seal came and said to the keeper of scales, 'Give me a part of the value of the seal, for I am in need.' The other man, because there had been no one around when he had given him the seal, dared to deny everything, saying, 'You did not give me anything.' As he went out, quite upset, the luminary encountered him and said, 'What is the matter with you?' And he told him the situation. And he said to him, 'Did you really give it to him?' He said to him, 'Yes.' The other replied, 'Say to him, "Come, give your word in St. Andrew's, and this will clear you." ' For there was a shrine to St. Andrew there. At the time he was going to make his oath, the luminary took his servant, went in to St. Andrew's, and said to his servant, 'Whatever I may do today, do not be alarmed, and remain calm.' Going into the shrine, he took off his clothes and began to conduct himself like someone possessed by a demon, yelling out mad sounds. And when the other two entered he said, 'The holy Andrew says, "Behold this wretch who took five hundred coins from the man and wants to deceive me." ' He then dashed over and choked the scale-keeper, saying, 'The holy Andrew says, "Give up the man's five hundred coins." ' The man, upset and frightened, confessed and said, 'I will bring them.' He replied, 'Bring them now.' So he left immediately and brought them, and the man who was truly inspired by the Lord said of the coins, 'The holy Andrew says, "Put six coins on the table." ' He put them there gladly. When they had left, the luminary put his clothes back on, conducted himself in a well-behaved manner, and went away to stroll by the scale house as usual. The keeper of scales, seeing him, scrutinized him carefully from head to toe. The luminary said to him, 'Why are you scrutinizing me, my friend? Believe that by God's grace I have no demon, but when the man gave you the seal, I was strolling by outside and I indeed heard and saw. If I had told you so, you would have said that one ought not to believe the witness of only one person. So I thought to perform this drama, so that you might not lose your soul, nor the man suffer unfairly the loss of what is his.'

IX (50) A brother went out to draw water from the river, found a woman washing clothes, and sinned with her. After committing the sin, he took the water and went back into his cell. The demons, having trodden him underfoot, tormented him through thoughts, saying, 'Where are you going now? Salvation is not yours, so why give up the world?' The brother, who realised that they sought to destroy him completely, said to the thoughts, 'Why do you come in after me and torment me to the point that I despair of myself? I did not sin; again I say, I did not sin.' He went off to his cell and pursued the hermit's life as before. The Lord revealed to an old man near him that there was a certain brother who, having fallen, then triumphed. The old man came to him and said to him, 'How are you?' And he said, 'I am well, abba.' The old man said to him, 'And do you suffer anything these days?' He said to him, 'Nothing.' The old man said,

'God revealed to me that you fell but then triumphed.' Then the brother told to him everything which had happened to him. And the old man said to him, 'Indeed, brother, your discernment has crushed the power of the enemy.'

X (51) A young man sought to renounce the world, and every time he would leave, his thoughts upset him and entangled him in worldly matters, for he was rich. One day when he was leaving they obsessed him and stirred up a great deal of dust in order to turn him back. Suddenly, having stripped and cast away his clothes, he ran naked to the monastery. The Lord revealed to an old man, 'Get up to receive my athlete.' The old man got up, met him, and learning the situation, marvelled and gave him the habit. Whenever people came to the old man to ask him about thoughts of various kinds he answered them, but if they asked about renunciation, he said, 'Ask the brother.'

XI (67) An old man said, 'There was an old man living in the desert who served God for many years and said, "Lord, let me know if I have pleased you." He saw an angel who said to him, "You have not yet become like the gardener in such and such a place." The old man marvelled and said to himself, "I will go off to the city to see both him and whatever it is that he does which surpasses my work and toil of all these years." And so the old man went and came to the place he had heard about from the angel, and found the man sitting and selling produce. He sat with him for the rest of the day, and as the man was leaving, the old man said to him, "Brother, can you give me shelter in your cell tonight?" The man was overcome with joy and welcomed him. Therefore they went to his cell and after the man had prepared things for the old man's refreshment, the old man said to him, "Have charity, brother, and tell me of your manner of life." Because the man did not want to speak of it the old man persisted for a great while in urging him to do so. Finally, having been shamed into it, the man said, "I usually eat late in the evening and when I finish, I set aside only what I need for my food, and the rest I give to those in need, and if I am host to any of God's servants, I give it to them. And when I get up in the morning, before I sit down to work, I say, 'This city, from the least to the greatest, will enter the kingdom because of their righteousness, but I alone will inherit punishment on account of my sins.' And again in the evening when I go to sleep, I say the same thing." When the old man heard this, he said to him, "This practice is good, but not so good as to surpass my labours of all these years." While they were getting ready to eat, the old man heard people in the street singing songs, for the cell of the gardener was in a public place. Therefore the old man said to him, "Brother, wanting as you do to live according to God, how do you remain in this place and not be troubled when you hear them singing these songs?" The man said, "I tell you, abba, I have never been troubled or scandalized." When he heard this, the old man said, "What, then, do you conceive in your heart whenever you hear these things?" And he said, "That they are all going to the kingdom." When he heard this, the old man marvelled and said, "This is the practice which surpasses my labour of all these years." In apology he said, "Forgive me, brother, I have not yet approached this standard." And, without having eaten, he withdrew again into the desert.'

3. MONKS SAVED BY WOMEN

There is a very little surviving material which describes the life of monastic women in the desert. It is known that they existed, and that their numbers were substantial. The literature which survives, however, is almost wholly about men, about abbas and their spiritual sons. Fortunately, monastic women have found the apophthegmata and related stories to be as inspiring to them as to monastic men. There remains, however, a problematic area, and that is the manner in which the desert men regarded women.

Celibacy is one of the ascetical renunciations which makes the monastic life possible. Because of the difficulties inherent in a monk's decision to live celibately, temptations to seek the visible (and tangible) rewards of sexual activity rather than less immediate spiritual goals are very real. The desert monks developed ways of facing and resisting such temptation and would teach these ways to their young disciples. The obvious, although unfortunate, method was to denounce marriage and sexuality, and to fix the blame for lustful passions upon demons and their female accomplices. (The few surviving sayings and stories about desert mothers reveal little about their methods of dealing with the same difficulties.) The more edifying, and probably more helpful, stories and sayings show how a tempted monk may come to recognize his confusion and then learn that self-knowledge can free him from his obsessions. The collection in Coislin 126 contains three unusual stories about women who helped monks towards this self-knowledge, and who strengthened rather than threatened monastic vocations. The stories portray how relations between the sexes can be creative and maturing, even for monks, rather than inevitably dangerous.

I (49) A brother was sent on an errand by his abbot, and arriving at a place which had water, he found a woman there washing clothes. Overcome, he asked her if he might sleep with her. She said to him, 'Listening to you is easy, but I could be the cause of great suffering for you.' He said to her, 'How?' She answered, 'After committing the deed, your conscience will strike you, and either you will give up on yourself, or it will require great effort for you to reach the state which is yours now: therefore, before you experience that hurt, go on your way in peace.' When he heard this he was struck with contrition and thanked both God and her wisdom. He went to his abbot, informed him of the event, and he too marvelled. And the brother urged the rest not to go out of the monastery, and so he himself remained in the monastery, not going out, until death.

II (52) Someone related, 'A brother living in a cenobium used to be sent on errands for the cenobium. There was a devout secular man in a certain town and he would receive him in faith whenever he went to the town. This secular had one daughter who was recently widowed, after two years of marriage. The brother was assaulted by desire for her as he would come and go. She, being intelligent, knew this and kept herself from appearing before him. One day her father went to the nearby city on an errand, and left her alone in the house. The brother came according to custom, found her alone, and said to her, "Where is your father?" She said to him, "He went to the city." The brother began to be agitated by the assault [of lust], and wanted to fall upon her. She thought quickly and said to him, "Do not be agitated, my father is not coming back for a while; here we are, just the two of us. I know that you monks do nothing without praying. Therefore stir yourself to pray to God, and if something occurs to you, we will do it." He did not want to pray, and was still agitated by the assault. She said to him, "Have you ever known a woman?" He said to her, "No, but for that very reason I want to find out what it is like." She said to him, "That is why you are so agitated, for you are unaware of the odour of suffering women." And, wanting to lessen his agony, she said, "You see, I am in my menses, and no one can come near me or smell me because of the odour." When he heard these things from her, and others like them, he was disgusted, came to his senses, and wept. When she saw that he had come to his senses, she said to him, "Look, if I had been persuaded by you, we would have already committed the sin. With what sort of face would you look upon my father, or go off to your monastery and hear the choir of those holy ones singing? Therefore I urge you from now on to be sober, and not to want to destroy those fruits of your labours because of a little weak pleasure, or to deprive yourself of an eternal good." Having heard these words from her, the suffering brother told them to me, the one who relates this, thanking God who by means of her wisdom and self-restraint did not allow him to be lost completely.'

III (84) One of the fathers related, 'There were two traders from Apamea [in Syria] who were friends and who traded abroad. One was wealthy, and the other was of moderate fortune. The wealthy man had a wife who was beautiful and also chaste, as events would prove. For when her husband died and the other man saw her worthiness, he wanted to take her to himself as his wife, but he was hesitant to speak to her, for fear that she would not accept. She was wise, and knew what was going on, and said to him, "Master Simeon,"—for this was his name—"I see that you are thinking about something: tell me what you feel and I will reassure you." At first he was hesitant to speak, but later he confessed to her, and pleaded with her to become his wife. She said to him, "If you do what I command you, I will accept." He said to her, "Whatever you command me, I will do." She said to him, "Go into your workshop and fast until I summon you, and in truth I will not eat anything until I call for you." He agreed, but she did not tell him a specific time when she would call for him.

He went off for one day, then a second, then a third, and still she did not call for him. But he persevered, either out of love for her or because God had arranged matters and provided him with endurance, having seen where he was going to call him: for after all this he became a vessel of election. On the fourth day, she sent for him. He had little strength, and being unable to come on foot due to his suffering, he had to be carried. She for her part prepared a table and a bed and said to him, "Look, here is a table and there is a bed: where do you wish to begin?" He said to her, "I implore you, have mercy on me, and give me a bit to eat because I am weak. For if it were to be a woman first, I would not be capable of it due to the feebleness afflicting me." Then she said to him, "See how when you were hungry you preferred food to me, to every woman, and to pleasure? Therefore, whenever you have such thoughts, make use of this medicine, and be free from every foul thought. For you have convinced me that after my husband, I shall marry neither you nor any other, but under the protection of Christ I hope to remain as I am, a widow." Then, struck with contrition and marvelling at her wisdom and self-restraint, he

31

said to her, "Since the Lord has seen fit to oversee my salvation by means of your wisdom, what do you advise me to do?" She, moved by his youth and beauty, and being careful lest at that moment she also might suffer such a temptation, said to him, "By God, I believe that you love no one more than me?" He said to her, "It is so." She said to him, "I, and this is God's truth, also love you, but since it is the voice of the Lord which says, 'If someone comes to me and does not hate his father and mother, and wife and children and brothers, and even his own life, he cannot be my disciple' [Lk 14:26], let us part from one another because of God, so that the Lord might consider you to have renounced your wife because of God, and I to have renounced my husband. For there is a monastery of hermits in our region at Apamea and if you are fully intending to be saved, become a monk there and you will truly please God." Immediately he gave up his trade, hastened to that monastery, and remained there until the time of his death. And he was esteemed, for he had a clean mind, saw things in a suitable manner, and regarded them spiritually.' All of these things Abbot Simeon himself related to the narrator.

4. STORIES ABOUT NATURAL BROTHERS

Another of the monastic renunciations was the break from parents and siblings. Two sayings of Jesus are often adduced to describe the monastic attitude towards family. The first is St. Luke's rather severe version, 'Anyone who comes to me and does not hate father and mother and wife and children and brothers and sisters, yes, and even his own life, cannot be my disciple' (Lk 14:26). The second is the gentler, but equally demanding, form found in St. Matthew: 'Anyone who loves father or mother more than me is not worthy of me; and anyone who loves son or daughter more than me is not worthy of me' (Matt. 10:37). Any interpreter of these words must remember that they are addressed to everyone who follows Jesus. The issue for any believer is one of priorities and perspective. Family obligations are always in tension with other duties: prayer, work, friendships. A monk is someone who has made a clear statement of priorities, and the renunciation of family means that the primary obligation of monastic profession must often assert itself against other ties. The desert literature reflects this tension. Often the attitude of the monks towards natural family can seem harsh; but so could that of Jesus. At times the problem was given an additional twist when two people from the same family would become monks. These stories about natural brothers who lived the monastic life together, or who were separated by that life, demonstrate that family ties can be a help or a hindrance in spiritual growth and that family conflicts and rivalries can follow the monk into the desert. As when dealing with the 'world', the monk's task with regard to family is not blind rejection, but a labour of insight and discernment.

I (4) There were two natural brothers who settled in Scetis, and it happened that one of them fell ill. Therefore his brother went to the church and asked the priest for communion. When the priest heard this, he said to the other brothers, 'Let us go to visit him.' They came to him, prayed, and left. The next Sunday, the priest asked the healthy brother how the sick one was doing. He answered, 'Pray for him.' Again the priest took all the brothers and went with them to the brother who was ill. After they had arrived and were seated, the sick man was about to die. The brothers started to argue, some of them saying that he was blessed with the Paraclete, and others disputing the point. Seeing this, the sick man's brother said to them, 'Why do you dispute with one another? Do you want to know who possesses the power [of the Spirit]?' Turning to his brother, he said to him, 'Are you going away, my brother?' And the sick man replied, 'Yes, so pray for me.' And the other said to him, 'My brother in nature, I could not let you depart before me.' Turning to the brothers seated there, he said, 'Give me a mat and a rug.' Taking them, he laid down his head, and he gave up his spirit first, followed then by the sick man. Immediately after the fathers had paid their last respects to the two of them, they joyfully brought them to be buried, for they had received the supernatural light.

II (5) There were two brothers who lived together in the desert. One of them once reminded himself of the judgement of God, and as a result ran away and wandered around in the desert for a long time. The other went out to look for him. After wearing himself out he found him, and said to him, 'Why did you run away like this? Did you alone commit all the sins of the world?' The other brother said to him, 'Do you think that I don't know that my sins have been forgiven? Indeed I know that God has taken away my sins, but I go to this trouble so that in the day of judgement I may come and behold those who are being judged.'

III (6) There were two brothers who were neighbours. One of them would hide whatever things he had, small change or morsels of bread, by putting them among his neighbour's effects. The other knew nothing of this, and marvelled that his possessions were multiplying. One day, however, he suddenly came upon him doing this, and took him to task, saying, 'By means of your fleshly concerns you have made a mockery of my spiritual concerns.' He exhorted him thus so that the other might no longer do this, and was reconciled with him.

IV (21) They used to say of an old man in the Cells that he was a recluse who did not go even to church. He had a brother according to the flesh living in another cell who fell ill and who sent for him so that he might see him before departing the body. His brother replied, 'I cannot come simply because it is my brother according to the flesh.' Again he sent for him, saying, 'Could you come tonight so that I may see you?' And his brother replied, 'I cannot if my heart is not found to be pure before God.' And he died and they did not see each other.

34

V (77) There were two natural brothers, and the devil came to separate them from one another. One day the younger lit the lamp, and the demon got involved and turned over the lampstand. The lamp also was overturned, and his brother struck him in anger. The other apologized, saying, 'Be patient, my brother, I will light it again.' And behold, the power of the Lord came and tormented the demon until morning. The demon went and told the one who ruled him what had occurred. The priest of the pagans heard the demon's tale and went off, became a monk, and from the start persevered in humility. And he used to say, 'Humility takes away all of the enemy's power,' just as he himself heard from the demon, 'When I agitate the monks, one of them turns around and apologizes, and destroys my power.'

5. STORIES ABOUT SIMPLICITY AND HUMILITY

One way of understanding the word 'monk' and its underlying Greek precursor, monos, is to interpret them to mean 'simple,' in the sense of uncomplicated, undistracted, single-minded. The other monastic attributes can be related to this primary characteristic; the renunciations make a life of simplicity genuinely possible (another understanding of 'monk' relates the term to 'single' in the sense of celibate), and monastic ascesis aims to develop an ability to see beyond complexity to simple truth. Foremost among the monastic virtues is humility, which is inseparable from simplicity, and which aims to cultivate a right sense of one's role within God's creation. The humility portrayed in these stories may seem naive or excessive, but it is not self-destructive or self-punishing. It enables the monk to begin to see and, when necessary, to speak. It is not a passive virtue, for it is the basis for charity. The remarkable quality of the desert monks' humility is the honesty it breeds: honesty about oneself, but also honest appraisals of others. If one who receives criticism must be humble, the one who speaks must be even more grounded in humility.

The desert has been considered by monastic tradition to be the ideal setting for a simple and single-minded search for God. The utter simplicity of the desert landscape itself, the lack of comforts and material distractions, the isolation from the complexity of human society, are all seen to create an atmosphere of simplicity where one may grow in humility and spiritual insight. The desert is not the only place for such labours, but its aptness is evident. As the Lord spoke through Hosea about Israel: 'Behold, I will allure her, and bring her into the wilderness, and speak tenderly to her... and there she shall answer as in the days of her youth' (Hos. 2:14–15).

I (14) Abba Zoilos, the presbyter of Tamiatheos, said that seven people gathered together to hear his father Abba Nathanael speak, and to imitate Abba Arsenios, and to stay in Scetis. Having renounced every worldly affair and undertaken these three things, they knew themselves to be worthless earthen vessels and said, 'This is how the great God sees us, and taking pity he will forgive our sins.'

II (28) One of the bishops visited the fathers in Scetis every year. A brother met him and brought him to his own cell, and after he set bread and salt before him said, 'Excuse me, lord, since I have nothing else to set before you.' The bishop replied, 'I wish that when I come again next year, I find not even salt.'

III (29) One of the brothers said, 'There was a discussion in the Egyptian *lavra* and all spoke, the great and the small, except for one alone who did not speak. When they had left, a brother asked him about it, saying, "Why didn't you speak?" Compelled by the brother, he replied, "Excuse me, for I said to my mind, 'If the mat under me does not speak, neither shall you speak.' And so I remained silent and did not speak out."'

IV (59) I heard concerning an old man, 'He lived in the temple at Clysma and did not do the work at hand, and not even if someone commanded him did he do it. So when it was time to work on nets, he worked on other things, and when they needed spinning he worked on linen, so that his mind would not be troubled by work.'

V (60) While the brothers were eating in the church of the Cells on Easter, they gave a cup of wine to a brother and insisted that he drink it. He said to them, 'Excuse me, fathers, for you did the same thing to me before and I suffered for a long time.'

VI (61) They used to say concerning an old man in the lowlands, 'He lived as a hermit, and a faithful secular served him. It happened that the secular's son fell ill. He pleaded many times with the old man, "Consent to come and pray for the child," and the old man rose and went off with him. The secular ran ahead and entered his house, saying, "Come and greet the anchorite." The old man, seeing from afar that they were coming with lamps, pondered, and then took off his clothes, jumped into the river, and began to bathe standing naked. When his servant saw this he was ashamed, and called to the people, saying, "Go back, for the old man has lost his wits." And going to him, he said to him, "Abba, why did you do this? Everybody was saying, 'The old man is possessed by a demon.'" And he said to him, "That is what I wanted to hear." '

VII (62) There was an anchorite who was grazing with the antelopes and who prayed to God, saying, 'Lord, teach me something more.'

And a voice came to him, saying, 'Go into this cenobium and do whatever they command you.' He went there and remained in the cenobium but did not know the work of the brothers. The young monks began to teach him the work of the brothers and would say to him, 'Do this, you idiot,' and, 'Do that, you old fool.' And suffering he prayed to God, saying, 'Lord, I do not know the work of men, send me back to the antelopes.' And having been freed by God, he went back into the country to graze with the antelopes.

VIII (71) A brother asked the old man abbot, 'How does someone become foolish for the Lord?' The old man said to him, 'There was a young man in a cenobium and he was given to a good old man so that the old man might love him and teach him the fear of God. And the old man would say to him, "Whenever someone humiliates you, bless him, and when you are seated at table, eat the nasty things and leave the good things, and if a garment is put before you to choose, leave the good one and take the worn one." The young man said to him, "Am I foolish because you tell me to do these things?" The old man said, "Rather, I tell you to do these things so that the Lord may make you wise." See how the old man showed why it is in the doing that someone becomes foolish for the Lord.'

6. STORIES ABOUT REPENTANCE, ILL-WILL AND PASSING JUDGEMENT

The renunciations described in the desert texts are the monastic form of repentance, the starting point of Christian growth. John the Baptist preached repentance in the Judaean desert, Jesus took up his cry, and the monastic tradition continued their emphasis upon taking responsibility for one's own life and submitting it to God for discernment. Such discernment generally relies on human agents, and lies at the heart of the relationship between abba and disciple. Because repentance is not a monastic prerogative, some of the stories in the manuscript concern non-monks who sin, realise what they have done, and make the moment the occasion of a turning away from sin and towards God. Closely allied with repentance in these accounts is humility, for it is humility that enables one to learn even from an apparently disastrous experience. For the wisdom of a monastic elder, of a friend, of a community to bear fruit, there must be a listener who is disposed to hear. On the other side, however, preaching repentance can easily become pronouncing judgement, and the desert monks were quite sensitive to this danger. Thus, the helpful quality of these stories is that they take the reader beyond the exhortation to repent and show the workings of grace through the simple power of example or a gentle word.

I (10) An old man said, 'This voice cries to humankind until the last breath: "Repent today!" '

II (11) Abba Theodotos said, 'If you live continently, do not judge one who lusts, for just like him you disobey the law. For the one who said, "Do not lust," also said, "Do not judge." '

III (13) They used to say of someone, 'He lived in a hermit's cell in Egypt and a brother and a virgin had the habit of visiting him. One day the two of them came to the old man at the same time. Seeing what was happening, the old man put down his mat and went to sleep in their midst. The brother was attacked by lust and fell on the virgin, and they sinned. The old man, knowing what had happened, said nothing to them. When morning came the old man sent them away, displaying none of his deep sadness. As they were going on their way they wondered together if the old man knew or not. They went back to the old man, repented, and said to him, "Abba, did you not know how Satan mocked us?" And he said to them, "Yes indeed."

They replied, "Where were your thoughts at the time?" And he said to them, "At the time, my mind was where Christ was crucified, and I was standing there weeping." And receiving a penance from the old man, they went away and became vessels of election.'

IV (20) There was an old man who each day ate three biscuits. A brother came to him and when they sat down to eat the old man set three biscuits before the brother. The old man saw that the brother needed more food and brought him three more biscuits. After they had their fill and got up, the old man condemned the brother and said to him, 'It is not right, brother, to serve the flesh.' The brother asked pardon and left. The next time the old man ate, he placed before himself three biscuits, as was his custom. He ate them and was still hungry although he restrained himself. Again the next day he withstood his hunger. The old man began to weaken and he knew that God had abandoned him. Prostrating himself before God with tears, he begged that he be not abandoned. Then he saw an angel who said to him, 'Because you condemned the brother, this has happened to you. Know therefore that the ability to deny the flesh or to do any good work is not within your power; rather, it is the goodness of God which strengthens you.'

V (31) There was a bishop in a city who by the working of the devil fell into fornication. One day during the synaxis in the church, with no one knowing of his sin, he confessed of his own accord before all of the people, saying, 'I have fallen into fornication.' He laid his pallium upon the altar, saying, 'No longer can I be your bishop.' All the people cried out, weeping and saying, 'Let this sin be upon us, only remain bishop.' In reply, he said, 'If you want me to remain bishop, do what I tell you.' Ordering the doors of the church to be shut he threw himself face down before one of the side doors and said, 'He has no part with God who while going out does not tread on me.' And after they did what he said, and the last one had left, a voice came from heaven saying: 'Because of his great humility, I have pardoned his sin.'

VI (32) There was another bishop in a certain city and it happened that he fell ill and all gave him up as lost. There was a monastery of women in that place, and the superior, knowing that the bishop was in a hopeless condition, took two sisters with her and went to visit him. And while the bishop was speaking with her, one of her charges who was standing by the foot of the bed touched his foot, wanting to know how he was. He was overcome by the touch, and called to the superior, saying, 'Since I receive no care from those nearest me, would you be willing to leave this sister with me so that she might care for me?' She suspected no evil and left her there. Empowered by the devil, he said to her, 'Make me a little boiled fish so I might eat.' And she did as he told her. After he ate, he said to her, 'Lie down with me, and conceive sin.'

Later, when she was with child, the clergy seized her, saying, 'Tell us who made you pregnant.' She did not want to confess. Then the bishop said, 'Let her go, for I committed this sin.' When he recovered from his illness, he went into the church and laid his pallium upon the altar. Going out he took a staff in his hand and went off to a monastery where he was unknown. The abbot of the monastery, being gifted with discernment, knew that the bishop was to come to the monastery and gave orders to the porter, saying, 'Watch, brother, for tomorrow a bishop will arrive.' The porter, thinking that he would come on a litter or with some of the trappings of a bishop, did not know the actual circumstances. Therefore the abbot went out to meet him, and greeted him saying, 'It is good that you came, lord bishop.' He was dumbfounded at being recognized, and wanted to flee to another monastery. The abbot said to him, 'Wherever you go, I will go with you.' After greatly comforting him, the abbot brought him into the monastery. Having truly repented, he died in peace, so much so that there were signs at his death.

VII (41) Two brothers who did not get on with one another were carried off to martrydom, and after being tortured were thrown into prison. One of them offered an apology to the other, saying, 'Because we shall die tomorrow, we should let go of the enmity between us and make peace'. But the other was not convinced. On the next day they were brought back once more to be tortured, and the one who had not accepted the apology broke down from the first attack. The governor said to him, 'Why did you not yield yesterday-when you were tortured in the same way?' The brother replied, saying, 'I have harboured ill-will towards my brother, and because I did not make peace with him, I have been denied consolation from God.'

VIII (43) A brother who lived in the Cells in Egypt shone because of his great humility. He had a promiscuous sister in the city who brought many souls to ruin. The old men often pestered the brother about her, and they were able to persuade him to go to her and somehow, by warning her, to stop sin occurring because of her. As he arrived in the place, one of her friends saw him, and went to tell her, announcing, 'Your brother is at the door.' She, deeply disturbed, left the customers whom she was serving, and at the sight of her brother jumped up with her head uncovered. She attempted to embrace him, but he said to her, 'My dear sister, save your own soul, for through you many have been lost. How will you endure sharp and eternal torture?' She began to tremble and said to him, 'Do you think that there is salvation for me after all this?' And he said to her, 'If you will it, there is salvation.' She cast herself at her brother's feet and begged him to take her with him into the desert. He said to her, 'Put your cloak over your head and follow me.' She said to him, 'Let us go now, for it is better for me to have my head uncovered and be unseemly than to enter the workshop of wickedness.' As they made their way, he urged her to repent. They saw some people coming to meet them, and he said to her, 'Since not everyone knows that you are my sister, go off a little ways from the road until they have passed by.' After a while, he called to her, 'Let us go on our way, sister.' When she did not answer him, he turned and found her dead. He saw that her footprints were bloody, for she had been barefoot.

The brother informed the old men of what had happened and they discussed it among themselves. God revealed to one old man concerning her, 'Since she cared nothing at all for the flesh, but scorned her own body and did not complain despite such a wound, on this account I have accepted her repentance.'

7. MONKS, DEMONS AND ANGELS

The two great stumbling-blocks for modern readers of desert literature are the harsh ascetical regimen practised by the monks and their apparent obsession with demons. Angels are easily accepted as signs or metaphors, and may even be considered rather quaint. But because this is an age which prides itself on having given up superstitions of all sorts—a pride with little actual foundation—demons are distasteful if not plain silly. Although ghosts and goblins have been jettisoned, there is today a great willingness to acknowledge the enormous complexity and powers of the human personality. A language has been developed for discussing psychological conditions and difficulties, with both popular and technical dialects. Related to and sometimes overlapping with this language are ethical notions of proper conduct and of deviations from what is socially or morally acceptable. In another age these notions were described as virtues and vices, and arranged in useful categories such as 'the three theological virtues' or 'the seven deadly sins.'

The ancients used the concept of demons in precisely the same way to explain otherwise inexplicable human behaviour. Along with the labelling came ways of dealing with such situations, and the methods employed against 'demons' often reveal a good if unsophisticated grasp of practical psychology. The troubles of the desert monks were not too different from those of today. However, the desert provided a stark backdrop for the actions of unhealed personality, and gave a dramatic edge to the work of recovering a sense of wholeness. The sharp awareness of sin and the dramatic vocabulary used to describe it should not mislead one into thinking that the desert monks were obsessed by evil and prone to superstition. They explained what they experienced in the vocabulary which lay at hand, and often with greater insight than those who casually employ the argot of psychology with little understanding of what they are saying.

I (12) Someone possessed by a demon came to Scetis and for a long time was not healed. One of the old men, being deeply moved, marked the demoniac with the sign of the cross and healed him. The demon, having been disturbed, said to the old man, 'Look, it was you who cast me out, so upon you shall I come.' The old man said to him, 'Come, I'll gladly have you.' The old man lived for twelve years with the demon and wore him out, for the old man ate nothing each day but twelve date pits. Finally the demon got free and left him. The old man, seeing the demon leave him, said, 'Why do you flee? Stay a while longer.' The demon answered him, 'God will bring you down, for it is he alone who can take you on.'

II (19) They used to say of an old man, 'He was walking in the desert and two angels accompanied him on his way, one on the right and one on the left. As they were going along they came upon a corpse by the road; the old man covered his nose because of the stench, and the angels did likewise. They went on a little way and the old man said to them, "Do you also smell these things?" And they replied, "No, for your sake we covered our noses. We do not smell the uncleanness of this world, nor does it come near us; but as for the souls that stink due to sins, those we can smell." '

III (33) There was an old man named Hierax in the region of the Thebaid who lived for about ninety years. The demons wanted for some time to cast him into *accedie* and beset him one day saying, 'What will you do, old man, for you have another fifty years to live?' In reply, he said to them, 'You have distressed me greatly, for I had been prepared to live for two hundred years.' And with great cries they left him.

IV (34) There was an anchorite in the region of the Jordan who fought for a good number of years. This man was deemed worthy of the grace of not receiving assaults from the enemy. He would even cast abuse on the devil in the presence of all those who came to him for his help, and he would say, 'The devil cannot do anything to those who fight if he does not find them to be like him, for it is the sordid who have always been enslaved to sin that he weakens.' The anchorite did not realise that he was protected by the help of God, and that it was because of this that he did not undergo assaults from the adversary. One day, with God's leave, the devil appeared to him face to face and said to him, 'What do you have against me, abba? Why do you dress me down with abuse? When have I greatly distressed you?' He spat back at him these words: 'Get behind me, Satan, for you can do nothing against the servants of Christ.' The devil spoke thus in reply: 'Yes, yes, but you have forty more years to live and I cannot find one hour in all those years to weaken you.' And, having tossed out the bait, he disappeared. Immediately the anchorite was plunged deep into thought and said to

44

himself, 'For so many years I have been here wearing myself out, and yet God wants me to live for forty more years? I shall leave and go into the world, and see those who are different from me, and associate with them for some years, and then come back and resume my ascesis.' He thought only about these things and resolved upon the deed. He set out and left his cell, and took to the road. He had not gone far when an angel of the Lord was sent to his aid and said to him, 'Where are you going, abba?' He said, 'To the city.' And the angel said to him, 'Return to your cell, and have nothing to do with Satan, for you have been deceived by him.' Coming to his senses, he returned to his cell. After three days had passed, he died.

V (35) A great anchorite said, 'Why do you fight me like this, Satan?' Satan heard and said, 'It is you who fight me so greatly.'

VI (36) An anchorite saw a demon urging another demon to go and awaken a sleeping monk. And he heard the other one say, 'I cannot do this, for one time when I awakened him he got up and burned me by singing psalms and praying.'

VII (45) An old man went to sell his woven baskets. A demon happened upon him and made the baskets invisible. The old man set himself to praying and was saying, 'I give thanks to you, God, for you have freed me from temptation.' The demon, unable to bear the old man's philosophy, cried out, saying, 'Here are your baskets, you evil old man.' The old man took them and sold them.

VIII (64) A monk was assaulted for a long time by the demon of fornication. In the synaxis he felt himself attacked, and taking no heed of being before the brothers, he stripped himself and tore away from the working of Satan, saying, 'Pray for me, because for fourteen years I have been so assaulted.' And because of his humility, the attack ceased.

IX (66) There was a presbyter from the Cells who was discerning. While coming into the church to complete the synaxis, he saw a number of demons outside the cell of one of the brothers. Some had taken the form of women who were speaking indecently, and others of blasphemous youths; others were dancing while still others were trying on different outfits. The old man sighed and said, 'The brother persists in negligence in every way, and because of it the wicked spirits surround his cell in this disorderly manner.' Therefore, when he had completed the synaxis, he returned and entered the cell of the brother, and said to him, 'I am suffering, brother. I have faith in you, and if you pray for me, God will completely relieve my heart from suffering. The disciple was shamed, and said, 'Father, I am not worthy to pray for you.' The old man persisted, pleading and saying, 'I will not leave unless you promise me that you will say one prayer for me every night.' The brother obeyed the old man's command. The old man did this because he wanted a new way to ensure that the brother would pray at night.

Therefore, when the brother rose in the night, he said the prayer for the old man. After finishing the prayer, he was struck with contrition, and said to himself, 'Wretched soul, you pray for the old man but you do not pray for yourself.' Therefore he offered one prayer for himself. He did this for a week, offering two prayers each night, one for the old man and one for himself.

On Sunday, while the old man was going to the church, he saw the demons once again standing outside the brother's cell, looking glum, and the old man knew that the demons were grieved because the brother prayed. He was filled with joy and went to the brother, saying 'Have charity and offer another prayer for me each night.' After saying the two prayers for the old man, he was struck again with contrition and said to himself, 'O miserable one, offer another prayer for yourself.' He did this for a whole week, offering four prayers each night.

When the old man came again, he saw the demons glum and silent, and gave thanks to God, and went in again to the brother and urged him to offer another prayer for him. The brother also offered one for himself, and said six prayers at night. When the old man came again to the brother, the demons were angry with the old man, furious about the salvation of the brother. The old man gave glory to God and after entering his cell and exhorting him not to be negligent but to pray unceasingly, let him alone. The demons, seeing the brother's perseverance in the prayers and in soberness, by the grace of God left him.

X (68) Someone related this, saying, 'In Scetis when the clerics celebrated the eucharist, an eagle would come down upon the sacrifice [cf. Matt. 24:28], and none of them would see it except for the clerics. Then one day a brother asked the deacon something and he said to him, "I do not have time for that now." When they went in for the sacrifice, the likeness of the eagle did not come as usual and the presbyter said to the deacon, "What is going on here, that the eagle did not appear as usual? Does the fault lie with me, or with you? Stand to the side, and if it descends, it will be known that it was because of you that it did not come down." And the deacon stood aside, and the eagle immediately descended. After finishing the synaxis the presbyter said to the deacon, "Tell me what you have done." He reassured him, saying, "I am unaware of having sinned, except that when a brother came and asked me something I told him, 'I have no time for that.' " And the presbyter said, "So, it was because of you that it did not descend, for the brother was aggrieved by you." And the deacon went away and apologized to the brother.'

8. DEATH IN THE DESERT

The ancients generally, and desert Christians especially, apprehended death much more vividly than do modern-day people. Western culture (at least in North American and Northern European varieties) has developed an elaborate system of funeral arrangements designed to minimize contact with the physical reality of death. Ancient peoples, like those of non-Western cultures of today, saw the fact of physical decay as part of the expected cycle of life and death. For Egyptians, the desert was especially related to death, for it was the place of burial, the abode of the dead, the realm of spirits and demons. Christians received from the Old Testament an ambivalence towards the desert as being on the one hand a place of trial or destruction, and on the other hand a place of encounter with God and of promise of salvation. This double perspective extended to the Christian view of death, embracing the reality of grief but in hope of new life.

The monks of the desert spoke of death as their call, a call to join the Lord. The stories below illustrate the different aspects of death in the desert: the calm acceptance, even welcoming of death by those confident in their hope; the manifestation of judgement upon those who died unprepared; the tender care extended to the dying by their monastic brothers. One can be sure that disciples grieved for their departed abbas, or that the old men mourned the younger ones who preceded them in death, but there was as well a faith which sustained life even in the midst of death.

I (7) A brother made a key and opened the cell of one of the old men and took his piece of bread. The old man wrote a note saying, 'Lord brother, whoever you are, be charitable and leave me half for my needs.' After dividing the piece of bread into two portions, he put out the note. The other entered again, ripped up the note, and took all the bread. After two years had passed he died but his spirit would not leave him. Then he called the old man and said, 'Pray for me, father. For it was I who took your piece of bread.' And the old man said, 'Why didn't you say so sooner?' At once he prayed and the other gave up his spirit.

II (8) A brother knew an old man, and seeing how wonderfully he cared for the dead, said to him, 'If I should die, will you care for me in the same way?' He replied, 'I will care for you in the same way, until you say, "Enough".' Not long after, the disciple died, and the old man's word was put into practice. Having cared for him reverently, the old man said to him in the presence of all, 'Have you been well cared for, child, or is there still a little bit remaining to do?' And the young man gave forth the reply, 'You have done well, father, for you have fulfilled your promise.'

III (23) A domestic servant became a monk and remained one for forty-five years, satisfied with salt, bread and water. After quite a while, his master felt compunction and he himself withdrew from the world and became a disciple of his own slave in great obedience. When the time of his death came he said to the old man, 'Abba, I see the powers coming to me, and because of your prayers they turn back again.' When the old man's death came, he saw one angel on the right and one on the left saying to him, 'Do you wish to come, abba, or should we go away?' And the old man said to them, 'I wish you to stay and take my spirit.' And thus he died.

IV (30) There was an old man who was sick, and since he did not have what he needed, a superior of the cenobium helped him and brought him relief. And he said to the brothers, 'Strain yourselves a little, so that we may bring relief to the sick one.' The one who was sick had a gold vessel, and after digging underneath where he lay, he hid it. It came to pass that he died and did not confess. After his burial the abbot said to the brothers, 'Take this bed out of here.' And as they pulled it up, they found the gold. The abbot said, 'If he didn't confess while he was alive, nor speak at his death, but put his hope in this, I will not touch it. Go, bury it with him.' And fire came down from heaven and for many days lay upon his tomb, in the sight of all, and all who saw, marvelled.

V (42) Another man, handed over to martyrdom by his female slave, when he was dying saw the slave who had betrayed him. Taking the gold ring which he wore, he gave it to her, saying, 'I give you thanks for having been for me the bearer of such good things.'

VI (63) Some seculars visited an anchorite and when he saw them he received them with joy, saying, 'The Lord sent you so that you would bury me. For my call is at hand, but for your benefit and that of other hearers, I shall tell you about my life. I, brothers, am a virgin in both body and soul, and up to now I have been inhumanly tempted by fornication. Indeed, as I speak to you, I behold the angels waiting to take my soul, and Satan meanwhile standing by and suggesting lustful thoughts to me.' Having said these things, he stretched himself out and died. While dressing him the seculars found that he was in fact a woman.

VII (74) A very pious monk beloved of God knew an anchorite whom he loved. The anchorite died, and entering his hermitage, the brother found fifty coins and began to wonder and to weep, afraid lest the anchorite might have offended God because of the money. Because he pleaded with God a good deal about this, he saw an angel of the Lord saying to him, 'Why do you lose heart this way about the anchorite? Leave what you are wondering about to the loving kindness of God. For if all were perfect, how would the loving kindness of God be shown?' The brother, having thus been reassured that the anchorite had been found worthy of mercy, became cheerful and gave glory to God from his whole heart.

VIII (88) Someone repented and became an ascetic. It happened that he immediately thereafter fell on a rock, hurt his foot, and shedding a great deal of blood became discouraged, and gave up his spirit. The demons came, wanting to take his spirit, and the angels said to them, 'Notice the rock and behold his blood which he shed for the Lord.' When the angels said this, his spirit was freed.

9. NAMED SAYINGS

One indication of the randomness of the Anonymous Series in Coislin 126 is the inclusion of some texts which refer to named individuals. Athanasius, the great bishop of Alexandria in the fourth century (d. 373), was a defender of the Nicene doctrine of the divinity of Christ, and a strong supporter of the monastic life. His biography of St Antony the Great, the first well-known Egyptian hermit, served as a kind of monastic charter both for the desert monks and for imitators elsewhere. St. Gregory of Nazianzus ('the Theologian' d. 389), was from Cappadocia in Asia Minor and was a friend of St. Basil the Great. Through his writings he advanced the doctrine of the Trinity and established the classical shape of Greek theology. Abbas Arsenios and Macarios the Great were among the most prominent of the desert monks; their sayings in the Alphabetical; Collection are numerous. Peter, martyred bishop of Alexandria (d. 311), was a great model for Egyptian Christians of the fourth century. St. Cyril, a later archbishop of Alexandria (d. 444), was a prominent controversialist and theologian of the divinity of Christ. The presence of these texts among anonymous monastic materials points to the importance the monks attached to communion with the larger church, as seen in its councils, bishops, and theologians.

I (1) Our holy father Athanasius, bishop of Alexandria, was asked, 'In what way is the Son the equal of the Father?' And he replied, 'In the way one sees with two eyes.'

II (2) Our holy father Gregory the Theologian was asked, 'In what way are the Son and the Holy Spirit the equals of the Father?' And he replied, 'The divine nature is like the one light from three suns standing together.'

III (3) The same said, 'God asks three things of all who are baptized: right belief from the soul, truth from the tongue, restraint from the body.'

IV (15) They used to say of Abba Arsenios that no one could keep up with the manner of his observance.

V (16) They said of Abba Macarios the Great, 'There was once a four-month period when he would go to visit a certain brother in Scetis every day and he never once found him resting. On one of his visits, he stood outside the door and heard the brother inside weeping and saying, "Lord, if your ears are not ringing from my crying to you, have mercy on me for my sins, for I do not tire of calling to you." '

VI (69) Some of the fathers used to say, 'When the holy Peter, archbishop of Alexandria [d. 312 in the persecution of Maximin Daia], was about to die, someone who had remained a virgin saw a vision and heard a voice saying, "Peter is first of the apostles, and Peter is the perfection of the martyrs." '

VII (70) A superior of a cenobium asked our holy father among the saints Cyril, the pope of Alexandria, 'Who are greater in observance, we who have brothers under us and direct each one in a different way to salvation, or those in the desert who save only themselves?' The pope answered, saying, 'Between Elijah and Moses, there can be no judgement, for both were pleasing to God.'

SECTION II
ANONYMOUS SAYINGS

T HIS category contains the anonymous sayings scattered throughout the first part of the manuscript, as well as the distinct series of forty-four *apophthegmata* which follows the stories in Section I. They are, with a few exceptions, pure apophthegmata, with scarcely any description of the scene or narrative line. Shorn as they are of excess verbiage they require little comment.

10. ANONYMOUS SAYINGS

I (24) An old man said, 'Joseph of Arimathea took the body of Jesus and placed it in a clean garment within a new tomb, which signifies a new humanity. Therefore let each one strive attentively not to sin so that he not mistreat the God who dwells with him and drive God away from his soul, for although manna was given to Israel to eat in the desert, to the true Israel was given the body of Christ.'

II (25) An old man said, ' "Bare your sword" ' [Judges 9:54], and the brother said, 'But my passions are not assaulting me.' And the old man replied, ' "Call on me in the day of your tribulation, and I will deliver you and you will glorify me." [Ps. 50:15]. Therefore, call on him, and he will deliver you from every temptation.'

III (40) One of the beloved of Christ who had the gift of mercy used to say, 'The one who is merciful ought to offer it in the same manner as the one who receives it: for such mercy is close to God.'

IV (54) Someone saw a young monk laughing, and said to him, 'Do not laugh, brother, since you are driving away from you the fear of God.'

Concerning the Habit of the Holy Monks:

V (55) The old men used to say, 'The cowl is a sign of innocence; the scapular a sign of the cross; the belt a sign of courage. Let us then conduct ourselves in a manner consonant with our habit, wearing all parts of it with zeal, so that we do not appear to be wearing an alien garment.'

VI (56) They used to say concerning an old man, 'While he was living in his cell a brother came by night to visit him, and heard him inside disputing and saying, "Oh, that's enough, get out," and then, "Come to me, friend." The brother entered and said to him, "Abba, to whom were you speaking?" And he said, "I was driving away my wicked thoughts and calling on the good ones." '

VII (57) A brother said to an old man, 'I see no warfare in my heart.' The old man said to him, 'You are a building open on all sides, and whoever wishes can pass through you and you are unaware of it. If you have a door, you should shut it, and not allow wicked thoughts to enter through it; for then you will see them standing outside and attacking you.'

VIII (58) An old man said, 'I lay the spindle down, and I place death before my eyes before I pick it up again.'

IX (65) An old man said, 'The root of all evil is forgetfulness.'

X (75) An old man said, 'If you want to live by the law of God, you will find the law-giver to be a helper.'

XI (76) He said also, 'If you want deliberately to disobey the commands of God, you will find the devil abetting your fall.'

XII (78) An old man said about the thought of fornication, 'We suffer these things from negligence, for if we were assured that God dwells in us, then we would let no foreign thing come upon us. For Christ the Lord, dwelling and abiding with us, beholds our life: wherefore we, bearing and beholding him, ought not to be careless but to make ourselves pure, just as he is pure.'

XIII (79) He said also, 'Let us stand upon the rock, and though the river may sprinkle us, do not fear and do not jump off, but sing calmly, saying, "Those who trust in the Lord are like Mount Zion. The one who dwells in Jerusalem will never be shaken [Ps. 125:1]." '

XIV (80) He said also, 'The enemy said to the Saviour, "I send my own to your own, so that I might upset them. And if I cannot act wickedly towards your elect ones, at least I can delude them during the night." The Saviour said to him, "If a child untimely born can inherit from his father, then can this be considered a sin for my elect ones?" '

XV (81) He said also, 'Because of you, Christ was begotten. The Son of God came that you might be saved. He became a child, he became a man, while being God. On one occasion he was a lector, for taking the Bible in the synagogue, he read, saying, "The spirit of the Lord is upon me, because of which he anointed me." [Lk 4:18]. He was a subdeacon, for "having made a whip out of cords, he drove out all from the temple, both sheep and cattle, and the rest" [Jn 2:15]. He was a deacon, for "having girded himself around the waist, he washed the feet of the brothers" [Jn 13:4,5,14]. He was a presbyter, for "having sat down in the middle of the elders [presbyters], he taught the people' [cf. Lk 2:46], He was a bishop, for "taking bread and having given praise, he gave it to his disciples" [cf. Matt. 26:26 and parallels]. He was scourged because of you, and because of him you bear no wrath. He was buried, and rose as God, arranging all things for us according to type and plan, so that he might save us. Let us be sober, let us be watchful, let us devote ourselves to prayer, let us make ourselves pleasing to him.'

XVI (86) A monk was working on a martyr's feast-day, and another monk saw him and said to him, 'Ought one to work today?' And he said to him, 'Today the servant of God went forth witnessing and was tortured. Ought not I, too, toil a bit at work today?'

XVII (87) An old man used to say, 'Every time the deacon says, "Give the kiss of peace to one another," I see the Holy Spirit in the mouths of the brothers.'

XVIII (89) An old man was asked, 'What is it necessary for the monk to be?' And he said, 'According to me, alone with the Alone.'

XIX (90) An old man was asked, 'Why am I afraid when I walk into the desert?' And he answered, 'Because you are still alive.'

XX (91) An old man was asked, 'What is it necessary to do to be saved?' He was making rope, and without looking up from the work, he replied, 'You are looking at it.'

XXI (92) An old man was asked, 'Why am I continually negligent?' And he answered, 'Because you have not seen the signs along the road.'

XXII (93) An old man was asked, 'What is the work of the monk?' And he answered, 'Discernment.'

XXIII (94) An old man was asked, 'From where does the temptation to fornication come to me?' And he answered, 'From eating and sleeping too much.'

XXIV (95) An old man was asked, 'What is it necessary for a monk to do?' And he answered, 'Practise everything that is good and avoid everything that is evil.'

XXV (96) The old men used to say, 'The mirror of the monk is prayer.'

XXVI (97) The old men used to say, 'There is nothing worse than passing judgement.'

XXVII (98) The old men used to say, 'The crown of the monk is humility.'

XXVIII (99) The old men used to say, 'Say to every thought which comes upon you, "Do you belong to us, or to our enemies?" and it will confess.'

XXIX (100) The old men used to say, 'The spirit is a well. If you dig, it will cleanse, but if you raise a bank over it, it will disappear.'

XXX (101) An old man said, 'I believe that God is not unjust for both releasing from prison and casting into prison.'

XXXI (102) An old man said, 'To drive oneself hard in everything is the way of God.'

XXXII (103) An old man said, 'Do not do anything before you ask your heart if what you are about to do is according to God.'

XXXIII (104) An old man said, 'When a monk stands in prayer, if he prays alone, he does not pray at all.'

XXXIV (105) An old man said, 'I spent twenty years fighting one thought, so now I see all people as one.'

XXXV (106) An old man said, 'Discernment is better than all of the virtues.'

XXXVI (107) An old man was asked, 'How does the soul acquire humility?' And he answered, 'When it is anxious about its own faults alone.'

XXXVII (108) An old man said, 'As the earth never falls down, neither does one who humbles himself.'

XXXVIII (109) An old man said, 'Whatever I have not been able to master I have not done again.'

XXXIX (110) An old man said, 'It is shameful for a monk to give up his possessions and leave his country because of God, and then to head off towards punishment.'

XL (111) The old men used to say, 'If you see a young man climbing toward heaven by his own will, grab his foot and pull him down, for it will be for his own good.'

XLI (112) An old man said, 'This generation is concerned not with today but with tomorrow.'

XLII (113) An old man said, 'Our work is to burn dead wood.'

XLIII (114) An old man said, 'Do not seek to be undespised.'

XLIV (115) An old man said, 'Humility neither becomes angry nor makes anyone angry.'

XLV (116) He said also, 'To sit happily in his cell fills the monk with good things.'

XLVI (117) An old man said, 'Woe to anyone whose name is greater than his work.'

XLVII (118) An old man said, 'Impudence and laughter are like a devouring fire among the reeds.'

XLVIII (119) An old man said, 'He who drives himself hard because of God is the equal of a confessor.'

XLIX (120) He said also, 'If someone becomes foolish for God, the Lord will make him wise.'

L (121) An old man said, 'Anyone who keeps death before his eyes at all times conquers despair.'

LI (122) An old man said, 'God investigates these things in us: mind, word, and deed.'

LII (123) The same said, 'We have need of these things: to fear the judgement of God, to hate sin, to love virtue, and to pray to God always.'

LIII (124) An old man said, 'Stay away from everyone who loves conflict in discussion.'

LIV (125) An old man said, 'Do not be friendly with a superior, nor have any exchange with a woman, nor be kind to a boy.'

LV (126) An old man said, 'Let us weep, brothers, and let our eyes bring forth tears, before we go to where our tears will burn our bodies.'

LVI (127) An old man said, 'Freedom from worry, with silence, and inner meditation beget purity.'

LVII (128) They used to say about an old man, 'He lived with brothers and would tell them once to do a task. If they did not do it, the old man stood up and did it without anger.'

LVIII (129) A brother asked an old man, saying, 'Is it good to have a rule about one's neighbours?' The old man said to him, 'Such rules don't have the power to break a horse's bit. You have a rule about your brother? If you want to have a rule, have one rather about passions.'

LIX (130) A brother hastening to the city asked a prayer of an old man. The old man said to him, 'Do not hasten towards the city, but hasten to flee the city and be saved.'

LX (131) An old man said, 'Someone who flees the world is like a dried bunch of grapes, and one in the midst of other people is like an unripe grape.'

LXI (132) An old man said, 'If you see me having a thought about someone, you also have it.'

SECTION III

'CONCERNING THE ANCHORITES'

THIS group of five stories is lodged in Coislin 126 between the run of terse *apophthegmata* in Section II of the Anonymous Series and the Systematic Collection of Section IV. The title, 'Concerning the Anchorites,' is quite general, but these stories clearly form an independent and probably later collection with its own distinctive features. They emphasize an extreme withdrawal from society and a severe asceticism which is different in spirit from most of the texts in the preceding sections (note the practice of renouncing clothes, and the grazing 'like the animals' by the monk in the fourth story; compare story VII in chapter 5, above). It is the sort of asceticism generally associated with the monks of Syria rather than of Egypt, although with the possible exception of the fourth story these are situated in Egypt or the Sinai. Some manuscripts contain only the first four stories; the fifth one stands apart from the rest and is more like the stories in the other collections. They are presented here in the sequence and position in which they appear in the manuscript.

11. CONCERNING THE ANCHORITES

I (132A) One of the anchorites told this to the brothers in Rhaithou [in Sinai], the place where there were seventy palm trees and where Moses stopped with the people when they came out of the land of Egypt. He spoke thus: 'I thought I would go into the inner desert on the chance that I might find someone who was living there before me and serving the Lord Christ. After travelling for four days and nights, I found a cave. Approaching it, I looked inside and saw a man seated. So I knocked, according to the custom of the monks, to make him come out and greet me. He did not move, for in fact he was dead. Unaware of this, I went in and touched his shoulder, and as I did so he crumbled into dust. I saw his tunic, and when I touched it, that too turned into nothing.

I was at quite a loss, and left there. I then found another cave and a human footprint. My hopes rose and I drew near to the cave. Again

I knocked, and no one answered; when I entered, I found no one. I then stood outside the cave and thought, "The servant of God has to come, wherever he may be." At the end of the day, I saw some antelopes coming, and the servant of God, naked. He had covered the unseemly parts of his body with his hair. As he came near me, he thought I was a spirit, and stopped to pray: he was, he said later, greatly tried by spirits. I realised this, and said to him, "I am a man, servant of God. See my footprints, and feel that I am flesh and blood." After his "Amen," he took a look at me and was reassured. Taking me into the cave, he said, "What brings you here?" I said, "I came into this desert to seek the servants of God. And I have not been disappointed in my wish." I then asked him, "How did you come to be here? How old are you, and how do you support yourself? And why are you naked rather than clothed?"

And he said, "I was in a cenobium in the Thebaid [in the south of Egypt]. I worked as a linen-maker. A thought entered my mind, saying, 'Go out and sit by yourself, and you will be able to find peace and to receive strangers and to earn a great income from your kind of work.' I heeded the thought and followed through on the deed, building a cell and doing work to order. I earned a great sum, and strove to distribute it to the poor and to strangers. But our enemy the devil was resentful as always, and entered into me with the intention of revenge, for I sought to offer the works to God. He saw a consecrated virgin order some items from me. I made them and gave them to her, and he then suggested to her that she order some other items from me. And so an acquaintance grew up between us, and with it increasing frankness. Finally there came touching of hands, and laughter, and eating together, and through such travail we brought forth sin. When I had lived with her in sin for six months, I thought, 'If I were to die today or tomorrow, I would have eternal punishment. For when someone seduces someone's wife, he is subjected to punishment and retribution; how much more the punishments deserved by someone who has seduced a handmaiden of Christ!' And so I ran off secretly into this desert, leaving everything to the woman.

I came here and found this cave and this stream, and the palm tree which bears me twelve palm branches a year. Every month it bears one branch, which supplies me for thirty days, and after that it bears a second one. After a long time my hair grew and my tunics wore out, and it seemed fitting to put my hair around part of the body." I asked him if in the beginning he had a difficult time there. He said, "In the beginning I suffered greatly, and lay ill on the ground due to liver trouble. I was unable to stand and complete the prayers of the synaxis, but lying there I cried out to the Most High. So there I was in the cave, in such great faintheartedness and pain that there seemed to be no future for me. Then I saw a man enter and stand near me, and he said to me: 'What is wrong with you?' And I replied weakly, 'I suffer in the liver,' and showed him the place. Joining the fingers of his hand together, he cut into the place like a sword and took out the liver. He showed me the wounds, and scraping with his hand, cast the stuff into a rag. And he put the liver back in, and closed the place with his hand, and said to me: 'Look, you are now well. Serve the Lord Christ as is fitting.' And ever since then I have passed my time here untiringly."

I begged him to let me live in the first cave, but he said, "You cannot bear the assaults of the demons." I was convinced by this, and asked him to pray before departing, and he prayed and then left. I have told you these things for your profit.'

II (132B) Another of the old men, one who had been found worthy to be bishop of Oxyrhynchus, related a story he attributed to someone else, although he was actually the one involved.

'I decided to go into the inner desert near the oasis in the region of the Mazices [the barbarian tribesmen who devastated Scetis in 407–08], to see if I could find some poor one serving Christ there. I took a few biscuits and enough water for four days' journey.

After travelling for four days, I ran out of food, and asked, "What shall I do now?" But I took courage, and resolved to continue for four more days unfed. But the body could no longer carry the burden of hunger and the weight of the journey, and I lost heart and lay down. Someone came along and touched my lips with his finger, just as a doctor will lightly pass over the eye with a probe. Immediately I felt restored, and as if I had neither travelled nor thirsted. As the strength returned to me, I got up and continued my journey into the desert. I continued for another four days, and again I was exhausted and raised my hands to heaven. And a man appeared, the one who had refreshed me before, and he restored me and I journeyed on for seventeen days.

Eventually I found monk's cell, a palm tree, water, and a man standing there. The hair on his head was completely white and served as his clothing. He looked afraid, and stood praying as he beheld me. He said the "Amen," realised I was a man, and touched my hand. He then asked me, "How have you come to be here? Is everything in the world still there? Are the persecutions still going on?" And I said, "It is thanks to you, who are serving the Lord Christ in truth, that I come into this desert. By the love of Christ the persecution has ended. Tell me now how you happened to come here." Lamenting bitterly, he began to say, "I was a bishop, and when the persecution occurred great punishments were brought to bear upon me. Eventually I sacrificed [to the image of the emperor] because I could no longer endure the torture. I recovered my senses and confessed my sin, and gave myself up to remaining in this desert until death. And so I have been living here for forty-nine years, confessing and beseeching God to forgive my sin, and the Lord has sustained my life with this palm tree. It was only this year, after forty-eight years, that I received assurance of pardon." After he said these things, he suddenly stood up, ran outside, and stood in prayer for many hours. When he finished, he returned to me. When I saw his face I was bewildered and afraid, for he had become like fire. He said to me, "Do not be afraid, for the Lord has sent you to prepare my body for burial." He finished speaking, extended his hands and feet, and died. I divided my tunic in two, keeping half for myself and using the other half to wrap the body of the holy one, which I then covered with earth. When I buried him, the palm tree withered and the cell collapsed. I prayed earnestly, begging God, "Leave me the palm tree, so that I can spend the rest of my days in this place." But this did not come about, and I told myself that it was not God's will.

I prayed and started off towards the inhabited regions. The man who had touched my lips appeared and restored me to health, and I returned to my brothers. I told them of it, urging them not to despair of themselves but to find God by patient endurance.'

III (132C) Two of the great old men were travelling in the desert of Scetis, and heard some muttering coming up out of the ground. The searched for the entrance to the cave, and when they found it they entered and found a holy old virgin lying there. They said to her, 'Why did you come here, old one? And who cares for you?', for they found no one in the cave except her alone lying ill. And she said, 'I have spent thirty-seven years in this cave, surviving on herbs and serving Christ. And I have not seen a man until today. God sent you so that you might bury my remains.' After she said this, she died. The old men glorified God, buried her body, and went away.

IV (132D) They said of a certain anchorite that he went into the desert with nothing but a tunic. After walking three days, he climbed up on a rock and saw grass down below, and a man grazing like the animals. He climbed down surreptitiously and grabbed him. The old man was naked, and was sickened because he could not bear the smell of human beings. He got free and fled. The brother went running after him, crying, 'I am pursuing you for the sake of God: wait for me.' And the other turned to him and said, 'And I am fleeing from you for the sake of God.' The brother cast off his tunic and followed him. When the old man saw that he had cast off his garment, he waited for him, and said when he had come near, 'You have cast from you the stuff of the world, and I will stand by you.' And the brother said, 'Father, give me a word by which I may be saved.' And he replied, 'Flee other people, and be silent, and you will be saved.'

V (132E) An old man who lived in the desert as a hermit thought that he had attained perfection in the virtues. He prayed to God, saying, 'Show me perfection of the soul, and I will do it.' God wanted to humble him in his thoughts, and said to him, 'Go to this archimandrite [a monastic superior], and do whatever he tells you.' Then God revealed to the archimandrite, before the other one came to him, 'Look, this hermit is coming to you; tell him to take a whip and go take care of your pigs.' When the old man came, he knocked on the door, and entered the archimandrite's presence. After they had greeted one another, they sat down. The hermit who had come said to him, 'Tell me what to do that I may be saved.' The other one said, 'You will do whatever I tell you?' And he replied, 'Certainly.' And he said to him, 'Then take a whip and go care for the pigs.' Those who had known the hermit or had heard about him, when they saw that he was taking care of the pigs, said, 'Have you seen that great hermit about whom we were hearing? He has lost his wits, and is possessed by a demon, and takes care of pigs.' When God saw his humility in patiently enduring the taunts of others, he commanded him to return to his home.

SUGGESTIONS FOR ADDITIONAL READING

Background

Peter Brown, *The World of Late Antiquity* (London: Harcourt Brace Jovanovich, 1971).

Henry Chadwick, *The Early Church,* The Pelican History of the Church, 1 (Harmondsworth, Middlesex: Penguin, 1967).

Derwas Chitty, *The Desert a City,* Birkbeck Lectures (Oxford, 1966; repr. Crestwood, New Jersey: St. Vladimir's Seminary Press, 1995).

H. G. Evelyn White, *The Monasteries of the Wadi'n Natrun: New Coptic texts from the Monastery of Saint Macarius,* Publications of the Metropolitan Museum of Art Egyptian Expedition, 2 (New York: Metropolitan Museum of Art, 1932).

E. R. Hardy, *Christian Egypt: Church and People: Christianity and Nationalism in the Patriarchate of Alexandria* (New York: OUP, 1952).

Apophthegmata in English

E. Wallis Budge, *The Wit and Wisdom of the Desert Fathers: The Syrian Version of the "Apophthegmata Patrum" by Ânân Îshô of Bêth Âbhê* (London: Oxford University Press, 1934) [Syriac Systematic Collection].

Owen Chadwick, *Western Asceticism,* Library of Christian classics, 12 (Philadelphia: Westminster Press, 1958) [portions of Latin Systematic Collection].

Benedicta Ward SLG, *The Sayings of the Desert Fathers* (London: Mowbray, 1975) [Greek Alphabetical Collection].

————, *The Wisdom of the Desert Fathers,* Fairacres Publications, 48 (Oxford: SLG Press, 1975) [Greek Systematic Collection].

Other Ancient Monastic Texts in English

Ammonas

Derwas Chitty and Sebastian Brock, trans., *The Letters of Ammonas, Successor of St. Antony,* Fairacres Publications, 72 (Oxford: SLG Press, 1979).

Antony

Derwas Chitty, trans., *The Letters of Saint Antony the Great*, Fairacres Publications, 50 (Oxford: SLG Press, 1975).

Athanasius

R. C. Gregg, trans., *Life of Antony*, Classics of Western Spirituality (New York: Paulist Press, 1980).

Basil the Great

W. K. Lowther Clarke, trans., 'The Longer and Shorter Rules' in *St Basil the Great: A Study in Monasticism* (Cambridge: CUP, 2013).

———, trans., *The Ascetic Works of St. Basil*, (London: SPCK, 1925).

Sr M. Monica Wagner, trans., *Saint Basil, Ascetical Works*, The Fathers of the Church (Washington: Catholic University of America Press, 1962).

John Cassian

Edgar Gibson, trans., *Institutes* and *Conferences*, (1894) in Nicene and Post-Nicene Fathers, Second Series (Edinburgh: T&T Clark, 1991).

Owen Chadwick, trans., *John Cassian: Conferences*, Classics of Western Spirituality, 7 (New York, Paulist Press, 1985).

Benedicta Ward SLG, trans., *Institutes* (London: Penguin, 2003).

John Climacus

Colm Luibheid and Norman Russell, trans., *The Ladder of Divine Ascent*, Classics of Western Spirituality (New York: Paulist Press, 1982).

Dorotheus of Gaza

Eric P. Wheeler, trans., *Discourses and Sayings*, Cistercian Studies Series, 33 (Kalamazoo: Cistercian Publications, 1977).

Evagrius Ponticus

John Eudes Bamberger, trans., *Praktikos and Chapters on Prayer*, Cistercian Studies Series, 4 (Kalamazoo: Cistercian Publications, 1972).

Desert Fathers

Historia Monachorum in Aegypte, trans. Norman Russell (London: Mowbray; Kalamazoo: Cistercian Publications, 1981).

Benedicta Ward SLG, *The Lives of the Desert Fathers*, Monastic Studies, 4 (London: Mowbray, 1981, repr. Piscataway: Gorgias Press, 2009).

Armand Veilleux, trans., 'Pachomius, Coptic and Greek *Lives* and other materials in the Pachomian corpus', in *Pachomian Koinonia* I–III, Cistercian Studies Series, 45–47 (Kalamazoo: Cistercian Publications, 1980–2).

Palladius

R. T. Meyer, trans., *The Lausiac History*, Ancient Christian Writers, 34 (Washington: The Newman Press, 1965).

Some Studies of the *Apophthegmata*

Richard Adam, 'Introducing the Apophthegmata', *Hallel* 5 (1977/78) 243–50.

Wilhelm Bousset, *Apophthegmata* (Tübingen, 1923).

Douglas Burton-Christie, *The Word in the Desert* (New York and Oxford: OUP, 1993).

Graham Gould, *The Desert Fathers on Monastic Community* (Oxford: OUP, 1993).

Jean-Claude Guy, *Recherches sur la tradition grecque des Apophthegmata Patrum*, Subsidia Hagiographa, 36 (Brussels: Société des Bollandistes, 1962).

Lucien Regnault, 'La priére continuelle 'monologistos' dans la littérature apophthegmatique', *Irénikon* 47 (1974), 467–93.

Columba Stewart OSB, 'The Portrayal of Women in the Sayings and Stories of the Desert', *Vox Benedictina* 2 (1985), 5–23.

——, 'The Desert Fathers on Radical Honesty about the Self', *Sobornost* 12 (1990), 25–39, 131–56; reprinted in *Vox Benedictina* 8 (1991) 7–53.

Benedicta Ward SLG, 'Apophthegmata Matrum', *Studia Patristica* 16:2 (1985), 63–6.

PATRISTICS TEXTS PUBLISHED BY SLG PRESS

Available from www.slgpress.co.uk

SLG PRESS PUBLICATIONS